360° sports

Thanks for your interest in exploring how to deepen the work of integrating faith in sport and ministry. This book represents well over 50 years of experience, interaction and analysis of what it takes to be a person of faith in the world of sport. I trust as you read the book you will make notes of your own journey and learning experience as you interact with the principles we've proposed and identified.

Please check out the 360**sports**.net website periodically for updates and new information or opportunities about how to be in dialogue with men and women around the world who are working to understand sport and faith in a very integrated, practical way.

Email us to share with us your response to Focus on **Sport** in Ministry so that we may learn with you from your insights as you process your own experience and perspectives with the materials presented in the book.

Sincerely,

Lowrie

Lowrie B. McCown
President, 360°**sports**

2501 E. Piedmont Rd. Suite 243 · Marietta, GA 30068 · 404.543.557 · Fax 770.575.5733 ·
www.360sports.net · info@360sports.net

360° sports©

Marietta, GA

FOCUS ON SPORT IN MINISTRY
©2003 by Lowrie McCown and Valerie J. Gin
All rights reserved. No part of this book may be reproduced or transmitted in any form or by any means, electronic or mechanical, including photocopying and recording, or by any information storage and retrieval system, without permission in writing from the publisher.

To contact us, write:

        360°sports©
        2501 E. Piedmont Rd., Suite 243
        Marietta, GA 30062   USA

or email us at: info@360sports.net

First printing, 2003

1 2 3 4 5 6 7 8 9 10 Printing/Year 07 06 05 04 03

ISBN 193261100-2

Cover design: Christine Richenburg

Interior design: Christine Richenburg

With *Focus on Sport in Ministry*, Lowrie and Val are pioneering new processes in ministry. This book will stimulate ministries to reach every corner of the World of Sport with the love of Christ simultaneously building a bridge over the dualistic chasm between spiritual and "secular" activities that currently exists. A ground-breaking work! Thank you for leading us into a whole new paradigm of thinking!

-Cassie Carstens, Chairman,
International Sports Coalition and President,
International Sports Leadership School

Lowrie McCown is a first generation pioneer in international sports ministry. His thinking has played a crucial part in the Gospel movement over the past 30 years. The collaboration of Val and Lowrie to publish these strategic principles is of vital importance to reaching the world of sport for Christ and the continued expansion of sport ministry.

-Andrew Wingfield Digby,
Chairman of Christians in Sport, United Kingdom

Without a doubt the most relevant book on Sports Evangelism and Sports Ministry to come out this year. This is a must-read. Flowing out of Lowrie and Val's years of experience and research, it is absolutely foundational for everyone involved in Sport and Recreation ministry.

-Dr. Greg Linville,
Executive Director CSRM,
Professor of Sports Ministry-Malone College

Sport ministry is an exponentially expanding movement in the world today. Lowrie is recognized as a strategic teacher in explaining where we are and where we can go in sport ministry. The concepts Lowrie and Val have outlined in this book, especially the McCown Sport in Ministry Map, are recognized in the International Sport Coalition movement as foundational for defining and designing sport ministry. I recommend this as a must-read book for anyone anywhere!

-Eddie Waxer, President,
World Sports International

"This book IS the next level of thinking for sport ministry. Lowrie and Val are presenting fresh biblical insights with critical strategic thinking concerning sport to raise vital questions so that lives will be changed and communities transformed in Christ."

-Peter King, Co Chair,
Quest Australia

Dedication

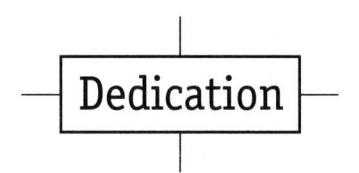

To my wife Randi, who sacrificially empowered me to serve the world of sport as a coach and teacher and to travel the world gathering the raw concepts and experience necessary for developing an integrated way of approaching sport in ministry.

To my children Taylor, Nathan, Hannah and Zachary, who have allowed me to enter their world as a father. Daily they teach me new perspectives through their own sport and faith journeys.

-Lowrie McCown

✟

To Mom and in loving memory of Dad.

"The righteous lead blameless lives; blessed are their children after them." Proverbs 20:7

-Valerie J. Gin

Authors

Lowrie McCown is the founder of 360° Sports®, fostering whole life ministry to the people of sport (athletes and coaches) worldwide. His experience as a player, a college and youth coach, a parent and sport ministry leader has led him to focus on addressing the issues related to sport and faith. Directing sports camps, serving coaches nationally and internationally, assisting Sport Federation and Olympic Committee leadership has provided fertile soil to germinate many of the thoughts and concepts presented in Focus on Sport in Ministry. Since 1991 Lowrie has been involved in the expansion of sport ministry worldwide serving as the Executive Director of the International Sport Coalition. Most recently Lowrie initiated sport ministry partnerships in eight countries and provided training to athletes, coaches, church and sport ministry leaders in over 120 countries as the International Executive Director of the Fellowship of Christian Athletes.

Valerie Gin is Associate Professor of Recreation and Leisure Studies at Gordon College. Val served 13 seasons as the Head Volleyball Coach and Senior Women's Administrator. She is among all-time win leaders in the history of Gordon sports. This past season Val was selected by the New England's Women's Volleyball Coaches Association and the Commonwealth Coast Conference as Coach of the Year. Val has held volleyball clinics in the U.S., Dominican Republic, Singapore, and has served as a consultant for the Honduran National teams. Val holds a doctoral degree in human movement from Boston University.

Contents

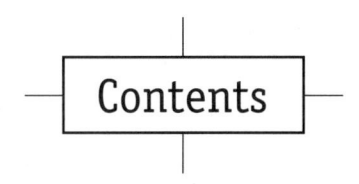

Introduction	11
Acknowledgments	15
1. A Sport-Eye View	19
2. A Biblical Perspective of Sport	33
3. Philosophical Perspective of Sport in Ministry	51
4. A Visual Perspective – The McCown Sport in Ministry Map	67
5. In the Cross Hairs - How to Use the Sport in Ministry Map	95
6. Past Perspectives and Trends in Sports Ministry	113
7. The Focus of Sport in Ministry	133
8. Sport Development: A New Perspective of Sport in Ministry	145
9. Adjusting Our Sights to the Frontiers of Sport in Ministry	161
Appendices / Case Statements	173
Notes	177

Introduction

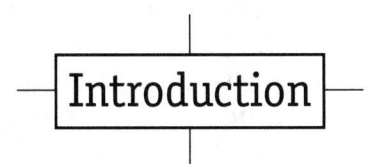

The principles and concepts addressed in this book have emerged from the authors' almost seventy years of combined experience both as players and coaches ourselves. As followers of Christ relating to sport, to sportspeople and to the world of sport, both of us repeatedly found ourselves wrestling with similar issues, feelings and questions related to sport and faith which were not traditionally addressed anywhere—not in the church, not in sport, not even in sports ministry. Simply put, we encountered a lack of meaningful dialogue or guidance (in sport) to help us in our thinking about sport and faith. In turn, it was our individual life stories and backgrounds—Lowrie McCown, as a sports ministry leader, and Valerie Gin, as a university coach and professor—together with time spent in study, questioning, analysis and discussion with sportspeople, students, sports ministry leaders and church leaders, that became the driving motivation prompting us to write this book. It is our hope that this book will help the reader(s) develop a clearer perspective of sport and faith.

As a result of our experiences and discussions, we have coined the term "sport in ministry" to give value to sport and the sport experience. With this new term, we propose that sport is the common ground for the integration of sport and faith. Sport and ministry have oftentimes been conceived as "either/or" propositions. That is, it is commonly believed that you can either do pure sport or pure ministry because they detract from each other. Our concept of "sport in ministry," however, suggests quite the opposite: sport and ministry can be seamlessly integrated as one. In other words, sport does not have to be put on hold in order to do ministry, nor is it necessary to put ministry on hold in order to do sport. The concept of sport in ministry presents a sport-valued approach to ministry. We believe that when the Presence of Christ is brought to the sport experience through the heart of believers, sport will be restored and the people of sport will be transformed!

A final note to our North American readers. This book is aimed at a global audience. We have intentionally written with this global context in mind, carefully selecting our terms and examples. For example, the term "sportsperson" is used instead of "athlete" since the former is the most commonly used term abroad. The use of the word "athlete" outside of North America is exclusive to track and field participants. Likewise, in this book we have preferred the word "trainer" over "coach." Also, the terms in the McCown Sport in Ministry Map, though newly coined and unfamiliar, have been developed from conversations with internationals the world over.

This book has been written by sportspeople with the sportsperson in mind. We believe that God highly values sport and the people of sport. As the Creator and Sustainer of the Universe, He gave humankind the intellect, physical abilities and resources to create and enjoy sport. The book's focus on sport has been shaped by these principles.

The first chapter gives a brief overview of the many definitions and/or conceptions of "sport" and speaks to the value of sport in ministry. The second chapter examines sport from a biblical perspective. Since we believe that God values sport, it is important for us to understand sport from God's perspective. The next chapter discusses the philosophy of sport in ministry; that is, how can we best proclaim, demonstrate, experience and integrate the gospel of Christ in the sport experience.

Chapter four introduces the McCown Sport in Ministry Map, a tool that provides a common language and perspective of sport in ministry. The Map helps identify the different areas of sports ministry, and also serves as an alignment tool for analysis and evaluation. Chapter five outlines how to use the Sport in Ministry Map to help you align where you and/or your ministry are in relationship to other sport ministries, and provides direction for keeping your focus on your target audience. Utilizing the Map, we give a cursory view of the history of sports ministry and the role of cultural influence in chapter seven.

After considering the past of sports ministry, chapter seven guides you to think where the focus of sport in ministry should be in the world today and in the future, posing the question, how can we analyze and shape sport in ministry in the future? In response, a new way of thinking about sport in ministry, called "sport development," is proposed in chapter eight. Sport development ministry encourages you to consider how to effectively minister to the people of sport through a relationship-based, sport-valued approach.

Lastly, chapter nine focuses on how the people of sport can be released to be the people of sport that God intends them to be. Sportspeople are free to be God's agents of redemption in the world of sport. Throughout the book, additional comments, quotes and illustrations have been set apart from the body of the main text. These highlight further concepts to consider, as do the process questions located at the end of each chapter. As you read, we hope you will be challenged to expand and clarify your own thinking about sport in ministry.

Please understand, however, that the concept of sport in ministry, like the aims of this book, is not a finished product, but a work in progress. This book must not be viewed as a program or a how-to book. Instead, Focus on Sport in Ministry has been written to stimulate the thinking and discussion about the role of sport in ministry from a traditional/historical context and to cast a vision for future opportunities and development. As authors, we are fellow travelers with you, seeking to understand sport and faith in the sport experience. It is for this reason, that when we use the pronoun "we" in the book, we wish to include ourselves with you, the reader, in the dialogue of sport, faith and ministry. We merely hope to raise questions, present new ways of thinking about and approaching sport in order to expand the powerful opportunities to reflect the love of Christ in sport.

It is our sincere prayer that this book will be a blessing to you. You may be a sportsperson (presently or formerly active), manager, trainer, coach, parent, sport doctor, sport biokineticist, sport psychologist, official, referee or sport ministry leader. No matter what your relationship to sport, as you process the thoughts inspired by this book, may they strengthen your faith, your love and perspective of sport, and may God expand your opportunities to serve Christ in the world of sport.

Lowrie McCown

Valerie J. Gin

Acknowledgments

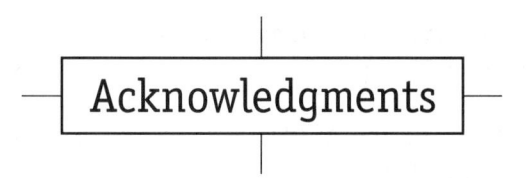

It is impossible to say thank you to the many people who, over the years, have nurtured and encouraged my thinking process, presenting challenging perspectives and engaging in sustained dialogue which led to this book. Nevertheless, I express my gratitude for the following:

The God-centered leadership of my mother and father Ed and Mary Irene McCown, who encouraged the development of an integrated perspective uniting faith and sport in a whole-life experience. They then released me and encouraged and supported my travels/work wherever the Lord called/led/sent.

My partners in ministry: Jim Welch of Summer's Best Two Weeks Camps; Wynn Lembright, Jack Roberts, Dal Shealy and Kevin Harlan, who gave me the opportunities to serve and lead through the ministry of the Fellowship of Christian Athletes (FCA); and Eddie Waxer of International Sports Coalition (ISC), who opened the sports ministry networks of the world. Many thanks to my brothers and sisters in the ISC sports ministry network who, over endless hours of coffee and international foods, challenged and prodded my perspectives of serving the people of sport for the sake of Christ.

Special thanks to Jim and Donna Wyland who have been like Barnabas to me over the past few years in navigating the waters in this journey in sports ministry.

Partners in sports ministry who have opened doors to teach and dialogue with leaders around the world through conferences around the world: the International Sport Leadership School, in South Africa; the Christians in Sport Academy in Cambridge, England, who assisted in deep refinement of the Sport in Ministry Map; and those co-workers with FCA who have joined me in the journey of deeper discovery to serve and release the people of sport to love and serve Christ in sport.

And, of course, my co-author, Dr. Valerie Gin, who shared her perspective of a coach/teacher and her gift of writing. She took on the unenviable task of compiling and drafting the manuscript from hours of dialogue and lectures so that the concepts could be shared with a broader audience around the world.

–Lowrie McCown

I would like to gratefully acknowledge:

My parents Clariese and David Gin for their godly examples. Thank you for generously and selflessly providing the opportunities, experiences, lessons and education that have enabled me to pursue my calling.

My older brother Phil who initiated my interest in sport...trying to keep up with him propelled my love of sport.

Dear friends Sonia and Jon Weston, without whose wisdom, expertise, time and editing, this book would never have come to fruition.

Gordon colleagues Jennifer Beatson and Ron Kay, who graciously spent hours of editing to restore the manuscript. Special thanks to Christy Richenburg who brilliantly put the manuscript into typeset.

The student athletes who allow me the awesome privilege of being their coach and professor. You have taught and challenged me to practice the presence of Christ on the court and in the classroom. I am also grateful to JoDee and Peter Herschend, who, from the beginning, supported my role/calling as a coach and my interest for sport in ministry.

Tammy Mentus, Mae and Louie Chan, Helen Soos, Jim Roberts and the late Calvin Thielman, who have lovingly mentored me in my faith journey. I would also like to acknowledge family and friends who faithfully support me in their daily prayers. Special thanks to Sandra Jordaan, Roy and Leora Tun, and Bob and Denise MacLeod for opening their homes to me as I worked on the manuscript.

Last, but not least, thanks to Lowrie McCown for introducing me to the world of sports ministry. Thank you for unselfishly sharing your passion and global vision for the people of sport.

-Valerie J. Gin

A Sport-Eye View
CHAPTER ONE

This is a book written by sportspeople with the sportsperson in mind. The authors believe that God values sport and the people of sport. For sports ministries to effectively minister to sportspeople in the new millennium it is vital that they value and understand sport and the role sport plays in the sportsperson's life. This introductory chapter seeks to answer the following questions:

+ What is sport?
+ How did sport originate?
+ What is the value of sport?
+ What is the value of sport in ministry?

What is Sport?

There are nearly as many definitions of sport as there are types of sports! To give an idea of the array of definitions posed, let us look at a broad definition followed by a detailed one:

+ "Sport involves four components: 1. Competitive Sport at all levels 2. Physical recreation: Non-competitive activities usually conducted on an informal basis, such as walking/hiking, cycling and boating 3. Aesthetic activities, such as movement and dance 4. Conditioning activities, engaged in primarily for health reasons and fitness benefits such as aerobics, weight training and exercise to music."[1]

✤ "Competitive activities or ceremonial games often involving foot races, wrestling, tests of strength, contests in accuracy of projectiles and dexterity with a ball, in accordance to a set of rules for purposes set apart from the serious, essential aspects of life for individuals or teams involving the whole human body acting independently, with a technical apparatus {i.e. sledding, sailing, auto racing, gymnastics etc.} or with animals {i.e. horse, calf or bull} derived from activities relating to 'the hunt' or 'preparation for war' as a basis for formal recreation and pacific contests in direct contrast to board games like chess or cards." [2]

In order to focus on sport in ministry, it is vital to have a common definition. For the purposes of this book, the authors have defined "sport" by the following five criteria (all criteria must be met)[3]:

✤ A competitive physical activity against an opponent(s) or self that involves the whole human body acting independently or with equipment designed for sport or animals; training is fundamental

✤ A winner is determined by score or a measurement of time, distance, or another specific goal—such as a flag, landmark, or capture of an animal

✤ An activity that is governed by a set of rules

✤ An activity that has a definite concluding point based either on time or pre-determined score or other ending point

✤ An activity that does not have the intent to hurt a person or animal

Note that this definition of sport does not include non-competitive leisure and fitness activities that utilize physical movements of the body. Non-competitive activities are wonderful recreational activities that have their value and place, but, in the authors' opinion, are not sport. Competitive activities such as board games or cards, mentioned in the second definition, are of significant value; however, they are considered games not sport. There is a distinct purpose for which the authors have crafted this definition of sport. Sportspeople playing, competing and thinking with this definition in mind have a whole different perspective of life and sport than a person who is engaged in physical activities for recreational, fitness or non-competitive purposes. It is important to keep this definition in mind, as it will come into play in latter chapters of the book. It is certainly not necessary for the reader to share the authors' perspective, but it is vitally important to recognize that this book is written with the perspective of the sportsperson in mind.

> Sports is the "magic elixir" that feeds personal identity while it nourishes the bonds of communal solidarity. Its myths transform children into their adult heroes while allowing adults to once again be children.
>
> Sports provides a "utopia of escape" that refreshes the partisan crowds and allows them to return with renewed vigor to their places in the political and social system.
>
> Escape into sports provided me with a place to go, a place of clear understanding and undeniable feelings.
>
> Sports is a sweaty Oz...an ultimate sanctuary, a university for the body, a community for the spirit, a place to hide that glows with the time of innocence when we believed that rules and boundaries were honored.[4]
>
> –Richard Lipsky
>
> Sports is life to the nth degree. It is life in extremis: every season you are born and you die, every forty minutes or nine innings you win and you lose. Every play encompasses an eternity.[5]
>
> –Neal Offen

> "Sports is life to the nth degree. It is life in extremis."

Where did Sport Come From?

Just as the definition and meaning of sport has evolved over time, a cursory historic look at sport will show how it evolved across different cultures through time. It is important to note the huge influence that cultures have had on the evolution of sport. Sport had its roots in the Primitive age as man refined his survival skills and abilities in hunting animals for food. Sport for entertainment can be traced back as early as 1788 BC to wrestling in China. In his two works, the Iliad and the Odyssey, which date from before 776 BC, Homer makes the earliest written reference to sport competitions. He details the funeral games held in honor of Patroclus, which included chariot racing, boxing, wrestling, foot races, and javelin and discus throwing.

During this time, the Greek city of Sparta dominated the region with their military fortitude. The focus of Spartan society was on physical strength and discipline. The Spartans were known not only for their military dominance, but also for their Olympic dominance. When Athens defeated Sparta in 480 BC, cultural ideals swung to an emphasis on the mind with a de-emphasis on the body. The Athens gymnasiums once built for disciplined exercise and training became places for philosophical debates rather than sport.

In the Roman Empire, the common themes of defeat and conquest had a direct effect on the types of sport played. There were over two hundred days of public holidays that supported the chariot races at the Circus Maximus. During this gory period the Coliseum hosted gladiators in spectacles against criminals, and Christians thrown to lions for entertainment. [6]

During the Medieval Age (500 to 1500 AD), sport continued to be violent as it paralleled the prevalent warring culture. Sport psychologists Thomas Tutko and Jeremy Tarcher describe the close link between war and games:

"Games have always been training for serious competition. The British, for example, were said to have won their wars on the playing fields of Eaton, where the officer class learned as children the importance of sacrificing to win. Games are sublimation of combat between individuals or between cities, regions, or countries. In the Middle Ages, some games were little more than ceremonial warfare, as when knights jousted-sometimes to death-or when the entire male population played a form of soccer in a no-holes-barred contest to move the ball into adversaries territory. Warfare metaphors still abound: competing sides alternately play "offense" or "defense," this team "destroyed" that one, so-and-so has a "killer instinct," a long pass is a "bomb," overtime play is "sudden death"[7]

It wasn't until the Renaissance and Reformation period (1450 to 1650) that educational proponents embraced the ideal of "sound mind, sound body," nurtured by sports such as archery, fencing, riding, and gymnastics. Nationalism in the late 1700-1800's led to the rise of running races, throwing events, dancing, and gymnastics as ways to fulfill individual needs for fitness and holistic character development while simultaneously developing and defending national pride.

The Industrial Revolution introduced a new era of sport since technological advances afforded people more leisure time. So, leisure games such as tennis, golf, lawn bowling and games of chance were born. (On an aside, it is interesting to note that the more leisure time a culture has, the more sport is embraced by that culture.) Social classes had direct effects on sport, setting up race and caste systems directly affecting the availability and opportunity for sport. The race and caste systems are still evident today. For example, in South Africa, sport traditionally follows racial and social class lines; that is, the blacks primarily play soccer, the browns for the most part play rugby, and the whites predominantly play cricket. But across the globe, huge efforts are being made to integrate and make sport available for all without regard to race or color.

During the period of mass production and mass consumption of the late 1800's came the birth of organized

> **The more leisure time a culture has, the more sport is embraced by that culture.**

competitive sport, most notably, cricket in England and Europe and baseball and basketball in the United States. Sport has grown by leaps and bounds since then. Today sport is played in every culture and on every continent. It is one of the most pervasive and provocative influences in our world. Sport is an intrinsic part of life and influences all spheres of society: family, community, economy, politics, media, education and religion.

Is Sport Good or Evil?

An institution as influential as sport cannot escape examination and subsequent judgment as either "good" or "evil". In many parts of the world, sport is thought to be inherently evil and participation in sports is considered sinful—an ideology that stems from ancient Greek thought. As mentioned earlier, in the historical war between Sparta, the Greek sports/warrior state, and Athens, the Greek religious and philosophical center, Athens defeated Sparta. The outcome of this battle gave rise to the Greek philosophy of secular dualism, or the sacred-secular divide, elevating the mind and spirit (sacred) as superior and the body (secular) as inferior. This pervasive cultural philosophy has even invaded Christian circles.

In contrast to this view, however, it is the authors' opinion that sport was designed by God and ordained by God, and, therefore, like all of His creation, was originally good. Similarly, the authors believe that God creatively made sportspeople who they are, intending them to lead rich, full lives enjoying what He has given while bringing Him pleasure. God intentionally genetically designed and wired some people with superior sport abilities. For many people, playing a sport is not merely an activity, but a vital part of who they are. Recognizing that God made some people with sport abilities and desires is an important point that should not be overlooked. Christians have felt the need to defend sport and sports participation with utilitarian purposes, such as a way to keep out of trouble, or for use in evangelism or character development. But these views overlook the idea that

> God intentionally genetically designed and wired some people with superior sport abilities.

perhaps God made players (athletes) with abilities simply for their enjoyment and pleasure.

The authors propose that sport is part of God's creation and is morally and ethically neutral. The morality of sport is not determined by the objectives of the activity itself, but by the heart of the participants. God gave humans the ability to create sport within His created order. He filled the hearts of players with the desire to play. Yet as a result of sin, sport, like everything else, is now in bondage to decay.[8] As redeemed people through faith in Jesus, we have the ability to restore sport as God intended. Our task as Christian people of sport is to play sport reflecting the image of Christ. That is, if sin has destroyed the good in sport, then perhaps the task of a Christian sportsperson is to reflect the image of Christ in the activity of sport so that sport can be played and enjoyed the way God intended. The following chapter will explore this concept in further detail.

Why People Play Sport

It is important to understand the motivation behind why people participate in sport to understand them better. People play sport for multiple reasons. It has been said that eight out of ten sportspeople play sport to have a healthy self-image. Some simply play for the love of competition. Many play to find a purpose in life. Others play to release stress, lose weight or improve their general health, to make friends, or to enjoy social recreation and entertainment. All of these represent healthy, positive attitudes toward sport. If people play for these positive reasons, there is a positive return from sport. Conversely, if people play for negative motivations, then there is a negative return from sport. The negative aspects of sport come directly from hearts of the people who play. One such example would be those people who are motivated to hurt or to impose power over others, thus damaging themselves, their opponents, the spectators and the sport itself. The converse is true, too: the positive aspects of sport stem out of the hearts and motivation of the people of sport who play.

> **If people play for positive reasons, there is a positive return for sport.**

Even if a sportsperson is playing sport to gain a healthy self-image, oftentimes he feels he must win or beat the opponent to feel good about himself. If his opponent is more skilled than he is, what can he do to win? This "positive" aspect of sport can quickly turn into a "negative" one. In fact, most negative aspects in sport come from unhealthy self-images. For when a person's identity is tied up in winning, he will do whatever it takes to protect his identity and win. Winning at all costs has stemmed from the need to have a positive self-image. Cheating, lying, making excuses, unnecessary rough play, blaming officials, violence, eating disorders and drug enhancements are all means he may take to ensure a win.

> "Competition in the best sense, is two opponents coming together to agree for the purpose of bringing out the best in each other, not the worst."

A sportsperson who is a believer should know exactly where his self-image comes from. His identity is found in Christ alone. He can compete with the complete freedom of knowing that his identity is not based on his performance. The late Latin, competere, of the word "compete" means to "come together to agree." Thus, "competition," in the best sense, is two opponents coming together to agree for the purpose of bringing the best out in each other, not the worst. The believer can play his best with the intent to win while viewing his opponent as a challenge to improve his abilities and skill. He does not view his opponent as the enemy, but as one who can bring out his best in all areas—physically through skills and fitness level; socially through his relationships with teammates, opponents and coaches; mentally through strategy and plays, spiritually through motivation and actions; and emotionally through self-control. He does not have to compete to defeat the opponent in order to feel good about himself; instead, he competes because of who he is. Thus, as believers in the world of sport, we have the opportunity to demonstrate our identity in Christ to people who are searching for healthy identities. What a strategic place and role the Christian competitor has as an agent of redemption in the world of sport!

Value of Sport in Life and Culture

Sport is of value not simply because God created it for the sportsperson to enjoy, but also because of its larger role in our lives and culture. Sport involves the whole person since physical, intellectual, social, emotional, and spiritual processes are all engaged when playing a sport. All components—body, mind, and heart of a player are fired up for action!

Furthermore, sport is a universal language across cultures. Sport transcends economic, race, gender, societal, political and religious barriers. You can go anywhere in the world and have common ground with people if you talk about sport and/or play a sport. While topics such as politics and religion should be avoided when starting a conversation or making new friends, sport, on the other hand, is almost always a safe subject for conversation. Moreover, sport is relevant to every culture. In most cultures, sport is highly valued. It has been said that the most popular and most scrutinized section of the newspaper is the sport section. More pages of the World Almanac are devoted to sports than to business, science or politics. The pervasiveness of sports is also seen by the majority of airtime that it occupies on radio and television stations around the world. In fact, there are now stations that carry sports 24 hours a day, and the web can now give play-by-play coverage of major sporting events anywhere at anytime in the world.

Sport also provides people with a common experience and a sense of belonging to a community. In this way, sport is a bridge that brings people together. Sport is enjoyed by people of all ages at different skill and competitive levels. Whether a Spectator or an Elite, most people have had some type of experience with sport. The simple fact that their children play sport together gives people a kinship they otherwise would not have. Cheering for the same team brings camaraderie to the crowd of Spectators. On a deeper level of connectedness, playing on a team provides a natural community of people with a common goal and interests. Sport has been called a "microcosm of life," entailing physical, emotional, mental, psychological, and spiritual challenges. These

> **Because of the life applications and challenges sport offers, it is an ideal environment for whole life discipleship!**

challenges are opportunities for the sportsperson to grow. Because of the life applications and challenges sport offers, it is an ideal environment for whole life discipleship!

Value of Sport for the People who Play

People of sport need to know that they are uniquely designed by their Creator, genetically wired to move, to crave competition, to be instinctively active, and to be energized by challenges. Since He was their Designer, God values the people of sport. Acts 17:24-28 states, "The God who made the world and everything in it is the Lord of heaven and earth and does not live in temples built by hands. And he is not served by human hands, as if he needed anything, because he himself gives all men life and breath and everything else. From one man he made every nation of men, that they should inhabit the whole earth; and he determined the times set for them and the exact places where they should live. God did this so that men would seek him and perhaps reach out for him and find him, though he is not far from each one of us. For in him we live and move and have our being."

From this quote, it is clear that God cannot be confined or limited to man-made buildings designated for worship. He can be found in all of His creation and in His created beings as well. In fact, according to Cassie Carstens, president of the International Sport Leadership School, "The sports fields of the world are becoming cathedrals to the glory of God!"

Participating in sport gives us an opportunity to acknowledge that everything we have comes from Him by utilizing the sporting talents He has gifted in us. Giving people gifts is enjoyable. Receiving a specially chosen gift brings great delight to the receiver. The giver is pleased especially when the special gift is utilized. In the same way, God has specifically chosen gifts for us. "He knit us in our mother's womb."[9] Every detail of our beings has been specially designed for us. God delights when we utilize, exercise and enjoy the gifts He has given to us. This is how we can glorify Him.

Irenaeus of Lyons wrote, "The glory of God is a human being fully alive..." A person who is fully alive utilizing all of her abilities and gifts is the expression of God's glory. The statement goes on to say that, "...the life of a human being consists in beholding God."[10] A person using and enjoying all her capabilities brings glory to God and is able to keep in mind her Creator. Enjoying God and the abundant life He has given us brings Him glory!

Being fully alive entails being wholly alive! Many of the trends in traditional sports ministry have followed a sole focus on evangelism at the expense of the *whole life* of a person reached through sport in ministry. The dualistic thinking that pervaded sports ministry in the past neglected the opportunity to holistically meet physical, social, emotional, intellectual and spiritual needs through the activity of sport. The authors propose, however, that the sport experience provides the ideal setting and environment in which to address holistic needs. Sport becomes a training ground for growth and maturity. The believer is challenged moment by moment to live out the presence of Christ amid the demands sport requires. Sport can also be an extensive breeding ground for not yet believers to experience the reality of the gospel. The lessons learned in sport transcend sport into all areas of life.

> **Sport is the common ground, the common approach to redeem sport and the people of sport.**

The Acts 17 passage also tells us that God is not served by human hands. That is, God does not need anything from us. He is the Creator and we are merely the created. It is amazing that God enables us to partner with Him as co-creators, giving us dominion over the earth. He does not need us or sport to bring others to Himself. Yet He allows us to have a part in enabling the spiritually dead to come to spiritual life. So, sport is not simply a tool for God to use, but a wonderful way in which we can glorify the Creator in our ministries by the way we appreciate how people of sport live, move, and are.

Value of Sport in Ministry

"Sport in ministry" is a term that the authors have coined to emphasize the value of sport and the sport experience. Sport

is the common ground, the common approach to redeem sport and the people of sport. Just as "the Word became flesh and dwelt among us,"[11] we, too, can dwell among the people of sport, thus bringing the presence of Christ in sport. The term "sport in ministry" conveys the idea that sport is totally integrated in ministry. Sport is not merely an add-on tool for evangelism. Many people try to justify sport, believing that it is a platform for evangelism. There is no doubt that sport can be an effective platform. But more importantly, *in and of itself* sport has value simply because God created people of sport who are wired to live, move, and be. Again, we are not de-valuing the ministry aspect, but emphasizing the fact that sport has worth in and of itself.

In this book, the terms "sports ministry" and "sport in ministry" have been used and are not meant to be synonymous. When the term "sports ministry" is used it refers to traditional ministries that use sport as a "hook" for evangelism. Sport is simply something to be used because it is an attractive platform for the gospel to be proclaimed. Sports ministry is sports evangelism. In sports ministry you disengage from sport to do ministry or disengage from ministry to play sport.

When the term "sport in ministry" is used it refers to a *sport-valued* approach to ministry. Sport in ministry is integrated in the activity of sport itself. It is the perspective that the demonstration of the gospel in the activity of sport is as valuable as what you say about the gospel.

> "Because humanity plays the key role in the order of God's world, human reconciliation will lead to the restoration of creation, just as human's sin led to creation's fall...God will eventually remake the world and its power structures so that they will reflect His glory instead of human arrogance...God plans for an eventual complete harmony, new heavens and new earth. All evil is to be destroyed through the cosmic results of the resurrection."[12]
>
> - N.T. Wright, Colossians and Ephesians

The authors contend that the people of sport need to be recognized and valued as people who need to grow towards and in Christ. In order to impact the world of sport we must value sport and take it seriously to redeem and transform the world of sport and the people of sport. The next chapter provides a biblical perspective of sport. It is imperative that we know how God views sport. The chapters that follow will detail this perspective of sport in ministry and the value it holds in this life and in the life to come.

Questions to think about:

1. Sport has been defined many different ways. How would a person who defines sport as competitive activity have a different perspective than someone who plays sport purely for socializing and exercise?

2. What value does sport hold for you?

3. Culture has had a tremendous influence on sport.
   How has today's culture influenced sport?
   How has the Christian culture influenced sport?

4. What influences you physically, mentally, socially, emotionally and spiritually when you are in the activity of sport? Can your value system be seen by the way you play sport or think about sport?

5. How did God genetically design and wire you?
   How can you utilize His gifts to bring Him glory?

6. How can sport bring out the "best" in a person?
   What in sport brings out the "worst" in a person?
   How can the heart of the participants reflect the image of Christ in sport?

A Biblical Perspective of Sport

CHAPTER TWO

What does the Bible have to say about sport? What role if any should sport play in our world? The authors believe that sport is birthed within God's created order. There are undeniably many problems in the world of sport. Could it be that the problem lies not in sport itself but rather in the hearts of the participants? We propose to answer these questions about sport from a biblical perspective by looking at God's plans for Creation and humankind.

The Bible has little to say directly about sport. Most of its direct references come from the writings of the Apostle Paul, who says that "physical training is of some value, but godliness has value for all things, holding promise for both the present life and the life to come."[1] Also, Paul consistently compares the Christian life to a race and encourages us to "run in such a way as to get the prize...a crown that will last forever."[2] The fact that the Bible has so little to say about sport, however, does not necessarily mean that God considers it unimportant. For example, the Old Testament has very little to say about the afterlife, even though the New Testament clearly shows that God cares deeply about this subject. During the four-hundred year Hebrew enslavement in Egypt, Egyptian culture was obsessed with the afterlife, as seen, for example, in the many pyramids built to preserve the Pharaohs' mummified remains and equip them

God's redemptive plan spans the entire width of Creation, including sport.

for life after death. The Old Testament's relative silence about the afterlife perhaps arises as a reaction by the Hebrews against this obsession with the afterlife too far. Similarly, perhaps the omission of sport from the biblical text was the Hebrews' response to the pagan culture around them. In this chapter we will begin by exploring God's original perfect design for Creation, how sin has broken and twisted this perfection, and God's plan for restoring His original design through Jesus. We will see that God's redemptive plan spans the entire width of Creation, including sport.

All Things were Created by Him and for Him

The apostle Paul writes, "For by Him all things were created: things in heaven and on earth, visible and invisible, whether thrones or powers or rulers or authorities; all things were created by Him and for Him. He is before all things, and in him all things hold together."[3] God created all things, all things were created for Him and all things are held together by Him. Paul was directly addressing the pervasive Greek dualistic belief of the day that the mind is pure and physical matter is evil. Paul speaks to this issue by stating that all things were "created by Him and for Him." Therefore, there is nothing made on heaven or on earth that is not a part of the created order—including sport. God created humankind with the intellect, ingenuity, creativity, abilities, instincts and resources to create sport.

God's Perfect Plan for Creation

The Bible's account of Creation in Genesis 1 concludes with the creation of humankind at the end of the sixth and last day of God's creative work. God blessed humanity with a unique and exalted place in Creation in that "God created man in His own image, in the image of God He created him; male and female created them."[4] Knowing that God created us in His own image and that God is a relational God, we understand that God designed us to be relational beings just like He is. In particular, God created humans with four vital and significant relationships: a relationship with God, a relationship with self, a relationship with other people, and a relationship with Creation.

Relationship with God. We were created to have an intimate relationship with God—so intimate that we bear His own image! No other creature has the same value God placed on humans by making us in His very own image. We were created for God's glory, "everyone who is called by my name, whom I created for my glory, whom I formed and made."[5] The Psalmist echoed God's value placed on us, "You (God) made him a little lower than the heavenly beings and crowned him with glory and honor. You made him ruler over the works of your hands."[6] We are not only created in God's image, but crowned with glory and honor, as well! Furthermore, in John's Gospel, Jesus calls believers his "friends."[7] Not only are we made in God's very own image, created for His glory, rulers over his creation, crowned with glory and honor, but regarded as His friends.

Relationship with Self. Secondly, in God's perfect plan each person was created to have a healthy relationship with himself—a relationship devoid of shame or guilt. "The man and his wife were both naked, and they felt no shame."[8] They were living in complete obedience to God and His intentions for them and were perfectly content. Adam and Eve's image was not based on what they did but simply on who God made them to be, the only created beings created in His likeness. The healthy image Adam and Eve enjoyed was enmeshed in knowing God's love, care and purpose for them. When God created humankind, He intended us to have a perfect relationship with God and with ourselves.

> **We are not only created in God's image, but crowned with glory and honor, as well!**

Relationship with Others. God also created us to have relationships with one another. "The Lord God said, 'It is not good for the man to be alone. I will make a helper suitable for him'"[9] So God provided Eve as a companion for Adam. He blessed their relationship and told them to "be fruitful and increase in number; fill the earth and subdue it."[10] Adam and Eve were created to provide help and companionship for each other and also to build community beyond themselves. In the same way God desires for us to have interdependent relationships, helping others and living in community together.

Relationship with Creation. Lastly, God created us to have a relationship with Creation. He commanded Adam and Eve to "rule over the fish of the sea and the birds of the air and over every living creature that moves on the ground."[11] He gave them dominion over Creation saying, "I give you every seed-bearing plant on the face of the whole earth and every tree that has fruit with seed in it. They will be yours for food."[12] God also "took the man and put him in the Garden of Eden to work it and take care of it."[13] In a literal sense, God gave Adam and Eve the responsibility to rule, fill, subdue and cultivate the Garden of Eden. In a broader sense, He intended for them to be stewards of all Creation—acting as developers of all the possibilities Creation had to offer. God lovingly placed humanity in a land that was blooming with possibilities to cultivate and enjoy, and gave us the ability to investigate, study, create, imagine, explore, design, and interact with what God created so that we could fulfill these stewardship responsibilities. Sport has grown out of the exercise of humankind's abilities and responsibilities as stewards and developers of God's created order.

> Sport has grown out of the exercise of humankind's abilities and responsibilities as stewards and developers of God's created order.

In order to preserve the integrity of the foundational relationships He designed, and to provide freedom to execute their responsibilities of stewardship and development of Creation, God's perfect structure for Creation established boundaries within which humankind should live and work. A story about children playing at a school playground serves as a good example of the need for and value of boundaries. The school was located on a busy street, well traveled by cars and trucks. Leery of the dangers posed by the heavy traffic, the children played very close to the school building, unable to enjoy the whole playground. Yet once a fence was built around the perimeter of the playground, the children played right up to the edge of the fence! Even though the fence set strict boundaries on the playground, these boundaries provided protection from the dangerous traffic on the street, giving the children freedom and safety to explore, experience and take pleasure in the whole playground. The same holds true for people. Though boundaries impose limits on our behavior, in so doing they also provide freedom to safely enjoy all that is within those boundaries.

Just as the town set up a fence to protect and thereby liberate the children on the playground, God set up boundaries to enable Adam and Eve to safely and freely enjoy the riches of His created order. God outlined the structure in which he intended Adam and Eve to live: "You are free to eat from any tree in the Garden, but you must not eat from the tree of the knowledge of good and evil, for when you eat of it you will surely die."[14] God designed a perfect Garden for Adam and Eve to explore, experience and enjoy within specific boundaries, but for their protection He placed the tree of the knowledge of good and evil outside these boundaries. Adam and Eve's life in the Garden provides a perfect picture of what God intended normalcy to be: walking with God in the cool of the evenings, caring for and exploring the Created order within the benevolent limits established by God, and living in peaceful unity with God, ourselves, others and the scope of Creation.

Broken Boundaries and Broken Relationships

What happened to this wonderful life within God's perfect plan? Instead of continuing to see God's boundaries as a safeguard for them, Adam and Eve were deceived by Satan into thinking that God set up the boundaries to keep something good from them. "You will not surely die," the serpent tempted Eve, "For God knows that when you eat of (the fruit from the tree of knowledge of good and evil) your eyes will be opened, and you will be like God, knowing good and evil."[15] Instead of continuing to trust God and respect the boundaries He established, first Eve and later Adam allowed themselves to be deceived: "When the woman saw that the fruit of the tree was good for food and pleasing to the eye, and also desirable for gaining wisdom, she took some and ate it. She also gave some to her husband, who was with her, and he ate it. Then the eyes of both of them were opened, and they realized they were naked; so they sewed fig leaves together and made coverings for themselves."[16]

What enticed Eve to eat? Eve's initial response to the serpent tells us that she and Adam knew the consequences of crossing this boundary. But Eve chose to believe Satan's lie that eating the fruit would make her like God. Merely being made in God's image was not enough for Eve—she wanted to *be* God. In the moment that she chose to eat, she stopped trusting that God had established this boundary for her good, deciding instead that He intended to deny her the ability to become His equal. So in that moment she chose to disobey God by stepping outside of His established boundaries and make up her own rules. Just like Eve, we too presume that God's rules for us are intended not for our good, but simply to prevent us from becoming like Him. So we continually choose to disobey God, attempting to dictate our own rules and determine our own right and wrong.

> **Sin has broken the foundational relationships in God's perfect design—with God, self, others and Creation—that He created us to enjoy.**

Disobedience, sin, is an act of rebellion against God's structure, in which we refuse to respect God's design and attempt to replace it with a design of our own. It is willfully taking glory from God and glorifying ourselves instead. This conscious act of disobedience against God and refusal to acknowledge His created order had and continues to have devastating effects on all of Creation. In particular, sin has broken the foundational relationships in God's perfect design—with God, self, others and Creation—that He created us to enjoy.

Broken Relationship with God. The moment Adam and Eve sinned, their relationship with God was broken. The first indication that this relationship was shattered came when God showed up to walk with Adam and Eve, and they hid because of their shame.[17] Because of sin they no longer had a perfect relationship with God; imperfect, sinful people cannot have a relationship with the perfect and holy God.

Humans overstepped God's boundaries when they refused to acknowledge God's sovereign order and rule in His Creation. The prophet Isaiah records God's words about Himself: "I am the Lord; that is my name! I will not give my glory to another."[18] Adam and Eve's refusal to give God the glory due to Him alone shattered the perfect relationship that the Creator had with His creatures.

Broken Relationship with Self. The moment Adam and Eve ate of the forbidden fruit, sin shattered the perfect image of God in which they were created: "Then the eyes of both of them were opened, and they realized they were naked; so they sewed fig leaves together and made coverings for themselves."[19] Adam and Eve were not aware of their nakedness or their own self-images until Satan came on the scene. Satan, unable to create original images, distorted the images God created them to have, twisting their healthy images to shamed-based images. A new schema, category of understanding, was formed because Adam and Even came into awareness of something that they were oblivious to. They never knew shame before they disobeyed God. Now instead of being perfectly content with who they are they are, Adam and Eve are ashamed and cover themselves.

Broken Relationship with Others. Adam and Eve's sin also damaged the perfect relationship that they had shared with each other. We see this clearly as the Bible's account of the Fall continues, "The Lord God called to the man, 'Where are you?'"[20] Adam answered, "I heard you in the garden, and I was afraid because I was naked; so I hid." God asked him, "Who told you that you were naked? Have you eaten from the tree that I commanded you not to eat from?" As soon as God asked Adam these questions, Adam was quick to blame his wife for what happened: "The woman you put here with me—she gave me some fruit from the tree, and I ate it."[21] What do you think that did to their relationship when Adam placed the blame on Eve? As Eve's protector and lover, he should have defended her and taken responsibility for his own actions, but instead he pointed his finger at her and told God that that the whole mess was her fault. What was once a perfect relationship was now scarred by sin.

> Where was Adam when the serpent tempted Eve? Why didn't he say anything? Eve was deceived by the snake, but Adam wasn't (I Timothy 2:14). He knew what was going on...He should have spoken up and said, "He's deceiving you into thinking you have more to gain by disobeying God than by remaining faithful to Him. That's a lie!" But Adam said nothing. He stood there, heard and watched the whole thing, and didn't say a word. He failed his woman. He failed, in his first spiritual struggle to represent God.[22]
>
> – Larry Crabb, *The Silence of Adam*

Not only did sin affect the relationship between Adam and Eve, it had a chain reaction on all human relationships. Just as Adam and Eve's disobedience scarred their marriage relationship, disobedience destroyed the relationship between their children and resulted in one brother killing the other. This tragedy grew from the same root issue—Cain disobeyed God's structure and plan for him and instead set up his own rules to govern his life. Cain killed Abel because he was angry that Abel had found favor with God and because he did not want to honor the rules God set up for him.[23]

Broken Relationship with Creation. The relationship that Adam and Eve enjoyed with Creation was also broken when they crossed the boundary God had established for them. God told Eve, "I will greatly increase your pains in childbearing; with pain you will give birth to children."[24] Likewise, God rebuked Adam, "Because you listened to your wife and ate from the tree about which I commanded you...Cursed is the ground because of you; through painful toil you will eat of it all the days of your life...by the sweat of your brow you will eat your food until you return to the ground, since from it you were taken; for dust you are and to dust you will return."[25] No longer would Adam and Eve live in joyful harmony with Creation; instead, he would have to wrestle with

---

Not only did sin affect the relationship between Adam and Eve, it had a chain reaction on all human relationships.

the cursed ground to produce food and she would endure great pain in childbirth.

Adam and Eve were given dominion over Creation to develop and explore the possibilities it contains. In disobedience against God's structure, though, they rejected His design and chose to live outside His plan and protection. Sin permeated every aspect of the future development of Creation from the time of Adam and Eve onward. The "ground is cursed"[26] because of sin and the "whole of creation continues to groan as in the pains of childbirth."[27] The problems caused by sin have only worsened as history has developed. The issues of selfishness, disobedience and conflict so evident in our present day ultimately derive from the same root decision as Eve made: we do not want to live within the structure of God's plans, so we foolishly reject ultimate freedom within God's structure and laws and choose instead to enslave ourselves to our own rules and structure. Sin continues to permeate Creation, resulting in brokenness, destruction and death, even as we continue to develop and explore Creation's potential in a manner twisted by sin that all too often perverts God's perfect design for Creation. Sin infects all of life—relationships, culture, politics, work, leisure and sport, and so on.

> **God's original design intended His creatures to live in perfect relationship with Him, each other and the rest of the created order.**

Worst of all, the Bible tells us that humankind on its own cannot repair the damage sin has caused. The apostle Paul describes humanity apart from God as "powerless,"[28] "prisoner(s) of sin,"[29] and "dead in (our) transgressions and sins."[30] Was life meant to be fractured and broken in this way? No! As we have seen, God's original design intended His creatures to live in perfect relationship with Him, each other and the rest of the created order. But throughout the ages humankind have resigned themselves to believe that brokenness of life is normal because they are no longer conscious of God's perfect plan. They have forgotten that brokenness was not God's intention for His Creation and do not realize that only God Himself can restore His created order and put things back together again.

God's Solution: Restoration through Redemption in Christ

God loves the world He created. He continues to value the structure and plan of His design, not out of duty or obligation, but out of love! God in His sovereign mercy does not leave humankind hopeless. The same God who through His awesome self-sufficient power called the Creation into existence can by that same power repair the damage wrought by sin and restore the Creation to His original intention. The New Testament reveals to us God's loving solution to the fall of Creation into sin: to restore His original perfect structure through the power of His redemptive plan—centered around Jesus Christ, "in Whom *all* things hold together."[31] Because of God's unfailing love for us, He sent His only Son, Jesus Christ, to pay the penalty for our sins by His death on the cross. God's demonstration of love through the gift of His only Son is the greatest affirmation to us that He has not given up on His Creation!

> God's demonstration of love through the gift of His only Son is the greatest affirmation to us that He has not given up on His Creation!

God's plan for repairing the brokenness of the world has its foundation in His only Son, Jesus Christ. God in human flesh in the person of Jesus came into the world as a human being so that He could redeem us (buy us back) from our slavery to sin.[32] As the apostle Peter reminds us, the price of our redemption was incredibly high—the shedding of His own precious blood through His death on the cross: "For you know that it was not with perishable things such as silver or gold that you were redeemed from the empty way of life handed down to you from your forefathers, but with the precious blood of Christ, a lamb without blemish or defect."[33] The target of God's redemptive work is the human heart. The Bible uses the word "heart" to represent the religious and moral center of a human being. "God declares Himself to the human heart through His revelation, and it is the response of the heart that determines whether a person will believe or reject God. This religious center determines the quality of a man's being and action."[34] Thus the redemption of a person's heart involves the transformation of that person's religious and moral center from one that is hardened in disobedience toward God, twisted by shame and guilt, and enslaved to sin and selfishness into one that is healed by forgiveness and set free to respond to God, self, others and Creation as God originally intended. Through redemption in Christ, we become members of His kingdom, in which God's perfect structure has been restored and the broken relationships with God, self, others and Creation have been made whole again through the transformation of the heart.

Restored Relationship with God. Our relationship with God is restored because He reconciled us to Himself through His Son, no longer counting our sins against us. The payment for sin is death, but God graciously paid our debt with His Son's own blood.[35] Each of us who believes that Christ died on the cross for our sins will not get what we deserve—death—but instead will inherit eternal life![36] Out of love and gratitude for this great gift that we cannot earn and do not deserve, we stop living for ourselves, following our own rules, and begin again to live for Christ.[37] Since redemption through Christ repairs our broken relationship with God, the sin-shattered pieces of God's image in our lives now come together to once again reflect His image in the world.

Restored Relationship with Self. The relationship with self is restored because "just as Christ was raised from the dead through the glory of the Father, we too may live a new life...If anyone is in Christ, he is a new creation; the old has gone, the new has come!"[38] Forgiveness relieves our shame and guilt. Through Christ we exchange our shame-based images for the glorious image of Christ in us.[39]

Restored relationship with Others. Our relationships with others are also restored in Christ. Jesus tells us, "A new command I give you: Love one another. As I have loved you, so you must love one another. All men will know that you are my disciples, if you love one another."[40] As recipients of God's love and forgiveness through the gift of Jesus Christ, we can now can "love one another deeply, from the heart"[41]—and through this godly love that we have for each other, men and women will know that we are His disciples. This restored ability to love will be a sign to our sinful world that God is love.

> **The Bible is the story of God reaching out to people as He attempts to restore the broken relationship.**

Restored relationship with Creation. Finally, our relationship with Creation is restored in Christ. Because we have been given fullness in Christ and all things were created by and for Him, our relationship with Creation is re-established.[42] Christ calls us as redeemed people to live our lives in obedience to Him by submitting to His rule and authority, which extends over all of Creation. We thus have the continued responsibility for its development and care, now no longer motivated by sin and selfishness, but by our desire to obey, praise and glorify God.

In His original perfect plan for Creation God gave human beings the privilege and responsibility of cultivating and developing Creation. Now that we have been restored to a right relationship with God through the redemption of our hearts we can now restore Creation to God's intended purposes. "All of life can be touched by the glory of the Lord saturated with God's presence" in the hearts of His redeemed children..."this is a mission of creation-wide proportions."[43]

> "Adam was built with a perfect design to live in a perfect relationship with God. Through his sin, this perfect relationship was broken and was irreparable by Adam. This also resulted in personal shame and fearfulness for Adam and Eve. The broken relationship between God and people is the theme of all Scripture. The Bible is the story of God reaching out to people as He attempts to restore the broken relationship...Grace heals the broken relationships with God and declares that we are whole and acceptable people."[44]
> –Donald Sloat, *Growing Up Holy and Wholly*

Restoration of Sport through the Hearts of Sportspeople

This mission of "creation-wide proportions" encompasses all of Creation. Redeemed people of sport have the ability and opportunity to restore sport the way God intended by restoring sport back to its proper relationship with God, self, others and Creation. God's children, as agents of redemption, can restore God's intended structure in sport through our hearts in the activity of sport.

Relationship with God restored in Sport. The Academy award-winning movie, Chariots of Fire, about the famous Scottish runner Eric Liddel, wonderfully illustrates four practical principles of how we can love, glorify and enjoy God through sport. Liddel was a Christian who had the ability of running fast. In one scene of the movie Eric's sister tries to convince him to give up running and follow the call to be a missionary in China. Liddel makes the decision to participate in the Olympics first and then go to China, defending his stance with the famous line "God made me fast. When I run, I feel His (God's) pleasure." The first principle of how to glorify God comes with Liddel's understanding and *acknowledgment that it was God who designed him* to be fast. He returns to God the glory and recognition as the Giver of this gift rather than taking credit for his speed. The second principle Eric's character demonstrates is *utilizing his God-given* gift—he runs! He chooses to be a faithful steward of the talent with which God has blessed him. The third principle is clear in Eric's *awareness that God is pleased* with him for enjoying the gift God has given to him when he states "I feel God's pleasure." This key scene, however, does not end there. Eric continues his speech explaining again his obligation to honor God by using his gift well: "If I don't run then I hold Him (God) in contempt." The fourth principle is closely related to the others. Eric understood that God made him with the ability to run fast for a *purpose*. That is, if he didn't run he would be denying what God created him to be.

> **As people of sport we have the opportunity to restore our relationship with God through sport.**

As people of sport we have the opportunity to restore our relationship with God through sport when we: *recognize* and give God glory for our gifts, when we *utilize* the gifts, when we *enjoy* the gifts God has given us—giving Him pleasure, and exercising our abilities fully by demonstrating who God created us to be. We have the wonderful opportunity to *give*

CHAPTER TWO

glory to God, Who is "in and through all things," who is Himself holding all our flesh, bones and organs, together. It was God who breathed in us His spirit giving us life. The apostle Paul said, "For in Him we live and move and have our being."[45] We have the ability to exercise, celebrate and enjoy who we are in Christ by acknowledging Him in our hearts through the activity of sport.

> **The battle in our own hearts is not between good and evil but between who receives the glory, the Creator or the created.**

Relationship with Self restored in Sport. Shame and guilt drive people to derive their self worth from their sport performance. As redeemed children of God we no longer need to feel guilt or shame. Our shattered self-images are restored with new ones in Christ: "since you have taken off your old self with its practices and have put on the new self, which is being renewed in knowledge in the image of its Creator."[46] Our sins are forgiven and the shame and guilt we experienced while in bondage is now replaced with the freedom that life in Jesus brings. Sportspeople can be image bearers of God once again, properly playing sport and enjoying the opportunity to design movements, strategize, and utilize God-given abilities, all of which bring glory to the Creator. Totally satisfied to find our identity in Him, we no longer compete to carve out an identity for ourselves or to glorify ourselves through actions and attitudes. This is how, in Christ, relationship with self is restored. Our self worth is in Christ alone. We play not to achieve mere accolades, but to play our best to glorify Him. In Christ we have the freedom to do our best regardless of the outcome. In Christ, sportspeople can accept responsibility for mistakes and forgive others for theirs.

Sport can be restored through the hearts of the people of sport when Jesus is set apart and recognized as Lord of the sport experience! The apostle Peter's instructions explain: "In your hearts set apart Christ as Lord, always be prepared to give an answer to everyone who asks you to give the reason for the hope that you have. But do this with gentleness and with respect, keeping a clear conscience, so that those who speak maliciously against your good behavior in Christ may be ashamed of their slander."⁴⁷ Not a moment of our lives is neutral; we either live for ourselves or for God. The battle in our own hearts is not between good and evil but between who receives the glory, the Creator or the created. Giving God glory means we have to humble ourselves in loving obedience to His rule and structure. When we do this we are free again to play on the whole playground, enjoying, discovering and exercising all the abilities and gifts He has given. The relationship with self is fully restored. We are free to be and to enjoy who God created us to be!

Relationship with Others restored in Sport. All of us are fallen, sinful people living in a broken world, yet we are restored through Christ to have healthy relationships with others. How can we restore our relationship with others through sport? Paul wrote the following instructions: "Therefore as God's chosen people, holy and dearly loved, clothe yourself with compassion, kindness, humility, gentleness and patience. Bear with each other and forgive whatever grievances you may have against one another. Forgive as the Lord forgave you."⁴⁸ As His children we bring redemption through our actions to the world around us as reflections of the holiness, humility, patience, forgiveness, and love of Christ.

> In sport, through our conduct, skill and expertise, we can model what sport was created to be.

The people of sport are best reached and influenced by other people of sport. In sport, through our conduct, skill and expertise, we can model what sport was created to be. We can live, play, and be a vital part of the sport community, demonstrating the reality of Christ in our lives. It is imperative that we take our responsibility of restoring the relationships of others in sport seriously. As we demonstrate to others how to play and enjoy sport as God intended, we are also responsible to have a role in restoring what sin perverted. What Satan cracked into pieces, we have the task of restoring. The broken, shattered images can once again reflect what they were intended to reflect: Christ. We will discuss this in further detail in chapters 7 and 8.

We also have the opportunities to identify and respect the image of God in others and share with them by the way we play and live. God is the Creator of life and talent. Our privilege and task is to play sport the way God intended, glorifying Him through the activity and help others in sport to do the same. Just as we can see God's glory in the beauty of nature, glimpses of God's image are also reflected in people who do not yet know Christ and through beautifully executed sport skills. All sports fans have watched a soccer player who scores a goal do a prideful cheer and dance. We have also seen a player score and immediately bow her head in prayer. Both players have executed wonderful skills, and we can acknowledge that both players' talents are gifts from their Creator. Pride does not have to ruin or discount the excellent display of sport abilities and the image of God it reflects. As believers, it is our responsibility to identify and acknowledge God as the Creator and Giver of these skills. We can play and watch sport, giving glory for the talent to the Creator, not to the created.

> It is up to us to redeem sport by honoring the Creator of sport and uphold sport to its proper biblical perspective.

Relationship with Creation restored in Sport. Because God loves the world, as stewards entrusted by God to cultivate and care for His world, we certainly cannot neglect or negate the part of the world called sport. The redeemed people of sport need to claim and recognize that God created sport. We must also identify the shattered images and be pro-active in restoring the broken pieces so that the world will know what God had in mind from the beginning. It is necessary that we play, teach sport, train (coach), and govern sport the way God intended sport to be. It is up to us to redeem sport by honoring the Creator of sport and uphold sport to its proper biblical perspective. Paul writes, "for everything God created is good and nothing is to be rejected if it is received with thanksgiving."[49] We are all called to develop and cultivate Creation. Our restoration mission of "creation-wide proportions" is the responsibility of all God's children. But it is the unique task and privilege of the sportsperson who loves Christ to reflect the image of God through play so that His Kingdom will be displayed on earth as it is in Heaven.

> "There is only one true Creator, only one who can speak into the darkness and the voice and cause a world to be, only one who can move upon the chaos and create order. He is the Lord God of Hosts. The rest can only mirror his creativity by arranging what He has already made in new and different ways. We create something out of something. He creates out of nothing...Satan has not created another world to vie with God's world, nor has he destroyed God's world. He took what God created as good and twisted it until it is slightly askew—until it gives glory to the created instead of the Creator. Our job, should we choose to accept it, is to take what the enemy has twisted and untwist it—to return it to its rightful position as that which gives glory to God. God wants us to sanctify the world, as we see it giving glory to him in all things. This is not only possible; it is essential. It is our mission in the world."[50]
> – John Fischer, *What on Earth are We Doing?*

In summary, if God created the world and everything that is in it and called it "good", then all creation is good by its very nature. The elements of sport are all contained within the created order that God deemed as "good". The problem is that humans disobeyed God causing all creation to suffer under the consequences of sin. What we see in sport that is not good is a result of human disobedience toward God. However, just as humans find restoration through Jesus paying the penalty of sin, the Creation becomes restored through the hearts of believers. Sport, too, is redeemed and restored through the hearts of the people of sport who demonstrate restoration through the activity of sport.

Questions to think about:

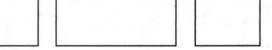

1. Do you think that the Bible's relative silence about sport indicates that God does not consider sport to be important? Why or why not?

2. What boundaries has God placed on your life as an athlete, a Christian, a family member, a spouse, and so on? In what ways do these boundaries limit you? In what ways do these boundaries free you to enjoy life within those boundaries?

3. Think back to one or more times when you disobeyed God. In retrospect, can you see that disobedience as being motivated by a belief that God (or an authority He placed in your life, such as your parents) was trying to keep some thing good from you? As you look back on the aftermath of the disobedience, do you see the wisdom of God's boundaries in that situation?

4. In what ways has humankind explored and developed Creation's potentialities in ways that honor God? What are some ways that humankind has continued to explore and develop Creation's potentialities in a manner twisted by sin?

5. In what ways has redemption through faith in Christ changed your view of yourself? Of others? Of sport?

6. In this chapter we have asserted that "our privilege and task as Christians is to play sport the way God intended." Since the goal of participating in a sporting match is to win, do you think that playing to win is part of playing the way God intended? What priority should the Christian person of sport place on winning?

Philosophical Perspective of Sport in Ministry

CHAPTER THREE

The ways in which we see, think, and act all stem from our philosophy of life. Whether we have integrated a biblical perspective of life as outlined in the previous chapter, each of us has a philosophy of life that frames how we interpret and apply our reality, our identity, our beliefs and our values. Accordingly, we design our lives around what we deem as important. Our activities of life become expressions of our perceived needs and interests.

A traditional philosophy of education is a helpful place to start in building a philosophy of how to minister to the people of sport. The following is an abbreviated, simplified perspective of how learners learn. The traditional perspective of education is that the teacher proclaims and the learner hears. The problem with this model is that the following communication cascade inevitably unfolds:

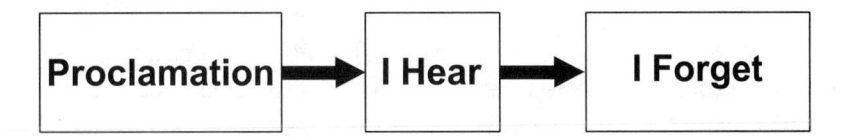

Proclamation → **I Hear** → **I Forget**

It has been said that:

- We hear half of what is said, (50%)
- We listen to half of that, (25%)
- We understand half of that, (12.5%)
- We believe half of that, (6.25%)
- And we remember half of that (3.125%)[1]

Unfortunately, most of what is said—a whopping 96.875%—is forgotten. We know this to be the case in sport. Simply having a trainer tell (proclaim) how to perform a skill does not mean the learner will know/understand or will recall how to perform the skill. If a tennis trainer only verbally explains to a novice how to execute a lob (a high arching shot into the opponent's backcourt), it is most likely that the novice will fail to comprehend and thus quickly forget what a lob is.

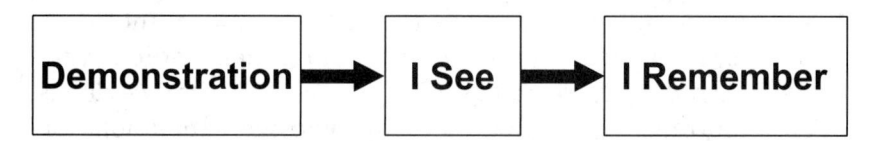

Demonstration → **I See** → **I Remember**

Since simply telling a learner how to do things is most likely to be forgotten, educators have concluded that *demonstrating* for them is key to their remembering. When a skill or information is demonstrated, the learner sees and he remembers.

In our tennis example, if the instructor explains and *demonstrates* how to execute a lob, the novice is able to see and identify the high arching shot to the opponent's backcourt as a lob.

Yet simply being able to recall and name something does not mean that the learner fully understands the concept, nor does it guarantee that he can replicate the skill. Visualizing a skill ensures neither comprehension nor execution.

In order for the learner to understand, he needs to *experience* by doing. Going back to our tennis example, when a novice is learning to lob a tennis ball he himself can attempt to lob the ball by mimicking the skill the instructor has demonstrated. The novice observes a lob executed by the trainer. He then imitates the actions performed by the trainer. He continues to practice hitting the ball with the racquet face angled up, aiming it so the ball lands deep on the other side of the court. The trainer gives helpful hints as the novice practices the lob. We now have a model of learning that leads to understanding as a result of doing:

Experience → **I Do** → **I Understand**

Nevertheless, we must go one step beyond this model in order to truly learn a concept. The final step of the learning process, then, is *integration* of the skill into the game itself. Experiencing and practicing the lob in tennis does not imply that the novice knows how to practically use the shot in a tennis match. For this level of learning, he needs to analyze and examine when the lob stroke is best used and why is it used. This step of integration brings an understanding of why a lob is used and an ability to utilize the lob at the right time. In our example, when the novice learns that the lob is a good strategic stroke for hitting an unattainable ball over an opponent who has charged the net, the learner can utilize this stroke at the appropriate times during the match. When he is able to integrate the skill into his game, he knows why the shot is appropriate and is able to *commit* to using it. In fact, integration, at its fullest, is when the player is able to execute a lob without even thinking about it because it is a natural part of his game. Therefore, this supreme model of learning is represented by:

Integration → **I Know Why** → **I Commit**

The integration level of learning is a trainer's greatest desire for the student. It is vital that players execute skills as part of strategic plays against opponents. They must understand how to apply and modify strategic plays, adapting them to game situations. They need to be able to think for themselves as they read situations and integrate the plays into the course of the game. In much the same way, if we want to train people of sport to grow towards Christ, and in Christ, we need to know the best ways to help them integrate biblical principles not only into their sport, but also into every area of their lives. The model of educational philosophy gives us helpful insights for arriving at a philosophy of sport in ministry.

> **The Four Laws of Learning**
>
> At the start of all your teaching,
> You would show me what to do.
> Always leading by example,
> DEMONSTRATION of "how to."
> Then you'd say, "Why don't you try it.
> I have shown you how to be."
> IMITATION—I attempted,
> As you watched me lovingly.
> "Do it this way. Do it that way.
> Try it once again like this."
> Your CORRECTION drilling habit,
> As we watched my skills progress.
> With occasional assistance,
> You retreated humbly.
> You were finished—I had learned it.
> REPETITION was the key.[2]
>
> -Swen Nater
> written about his Coach John Wooden

FOUR ELEMENTS OF THE PHILOSOPHY OF SPORT IN MINISTRY

The philosophy of sport in ministry utilizes the four levels of learning taken from educational philosophy: proclamation, demonstration, experience and integration. We will explore each of these four elements and learn how they build the foundation of the philosophy of sport in ministry.

Proclamation

Proclamation is proclaiming the truth of the gospel for people to hear. Proclamation of the gospel is necessary to provide the foundation of truth and to teach how the gospel is relevant in people's lives. A common method of teaching is a didactic approach, where the teacher lectures to students. It is a one-way style of teaching, the teacher proclaiming truth to the student.

Historically speaking, sports ministry has utilized the proclamation approach extensively. But unfortunately, this has been the only method used. In today's culture, mere declaration of the word of God may not be enough. People need to validate truth for themselves through experiencing it for themselves.

Bait and Switch. For example, in sports evangelism, we use sport as a "hook" to entice people to hear to the gospel. At many sports camps, sports are played to attract the youth to attend, but the "real" ministry occurs when the evangelist speaks at the evening program. Sport is simply the proverbial "hook" to catch the "fish" so the gospel, Christ in Word, can be proclaimed. We "bait" the sportsperson by offering what they would be interested in—a sports camp—and then "switch" by giving them what we think they need. The main emphasis of sports evangelism is not sport but using sport as a means to an end. If proclamation is the only element of the philosophy of sport in ministry utilized, then the following is the result:

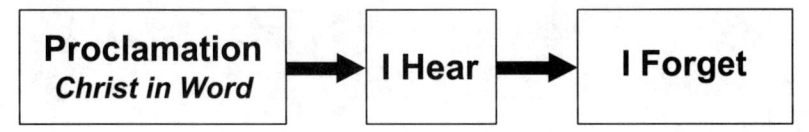

Proclamation *Christ in Word* → **I Hear** → **I Forget**

Demonstration

> People of sport who love God are able to demonstrate the word of God in action through their sport.

Another method of teaching is an approach where the teacher walks alongside learners as they go through life, helping them think through their decisions. This method implies a discipleship relationship where teacher and students unfold the truth in the reality and application of life. The teacher shares her life with students, thus demonstrating truth in action. People of sport who love God are able to demonstrate the word of God in action through their sport. Just as "the Word became flesh and dwelt among us," the people of sport can demonstrate Christ in action (become flesh) in the world of sport (dwell among others), with the following result:

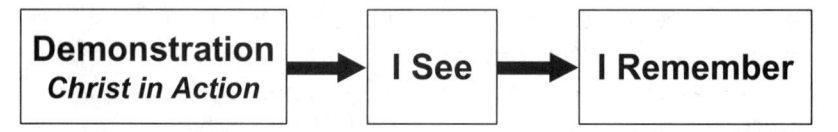

Demonstration *Christ in Action* → **I See** → **I Remember**

> I'd rather see a sermon,
> Than to hear one any day,
> I'd rather one would walk with me,
> Than point the way.
>
> The eye is a better pupil,
> And more willing than the ear,
> Fine council is confusing,
> But examples are always clear.
>
> The best of all God's creatures,
> Are the ones who live their Creed.
> To see good just in action
> Is what everybody needs.
>
> Though an abled speaker charms me,
> "I say,"
> I'd rather see a sermon
> Than to hear one any day.

Love demonstrated through everyday life. Paul, Silas, and Timothy demonstrated the gospel of Christ to the Church at Thessalonica as they lived among them. They describe their relationship to the Thessalonians this way: "We loved you so much that we were delighted to share with you not only the gospel of God but our lives as well, because you had become so dear to us."[3] Love motivated them to share their lives with them "not simply with words, but also with power, with the Holy Spirit and with deep conviction. You know how we lived among you for your sake. You became imitators of us and of the Lord; in spite of severe suffering, you welcomed the message with the joy given by the Holy Spirit. And so you became a model to all the believers in Macedonia and Achaia."[4] The people in Thessalonica received love from Paul, Silas, and Timothy through hearing the gospel and seeing it demonstrated in their lives.

> John Wooden, former basketball coach at UCLA, had a favorite expression, "No written word, no spoken plea, can teach our youth what they should be. Nor all the books on all the shelves: It's what the teachers are themselves."[5]

Just like Paul, Silas, and Timothy, we have the opportunity to show the love of Christ in the manner in which we live. Using the example of the sports camp, instead of thinking of ministry as just proclamation in the evening program, the Word of God should be demonstrated in all aspects of the camp: in drills, in scrimmages, during breaks, at meals, all the while demonstrating for campers the truth of the gospel by words and actions. Showing joy during exercises, patiently teaching players during drills, modeling self-control during games, are just a few ways we can demonstrate Christ in the activity of sport. Expressing to people the love of Christ in our actions clearly demonstrates the relevancy of the gospel in all of life.

Expressing to people the love of Christ in our actions clearly demonstrates the relevancy of the gospel in all of life.

Doing flows from Being. It is important to note that our ability to demonstrate the gospel is an outgrowth of our relationship with Christ. Who we are in Christ—our love and devotion to Him—supernaturally spills over into whatever we do. Jesus refers to this concept when He says, "If anyone is thirsty, let him come to Me and drink. Whoever believes in Me," as Scripture has said, "streams of living water will flow from within him."[6] When we come to drink and then believe in the living water, we are filled with and empowered by the Holy Spirit. The Spirit then flows over into our lives, bearing witness of our restored relationship to God. So wherever we are, because of who we are in Christ, we are able to demonstrate the reality of Christ in our lives.

> **"The Christian life is a love affair of the heart."**

Demonstrating the gospel is not a legalistic code of conduct, but a perspective of life based on one's relationship to God. It isn't a matter of doing the right things but of being in a right relationship with God. In other words, it isn't a matter of doing but of being. We are able to have a right relationship with God not because of anything we have done, but because of who Christ is. During Jesus' time on earth, He demonstrated to those around Him how to live a life reflecting God's glory. The strength of His ministry was based on His relationship to God. His example of being in right relationship of God models for us the need to be in right relationship with Him and His Father. From such a relationship we, too, will find strength for ministry. Just as Christ reflected God's glory, our demonstration of the gospel, being Christ in action, will reflect who He is and they will remember.

> "At one point in my own spiritual pilgrimage, I stopped to ask myself this question: "What is it that I am supposed to be *doing* to live the spiritual life in any way that is both truthful and passionately alive?...For above all else, the Christian life is a love affair of the heart. It cannot be lived primarily as a set of principles or ethics. It cannot be managed with steps and programs. It cannot be lived exclusively as a moral code leading to righteousness...The truth of the Gospel is intended to free us to love God and others with our whole heart. When we ignore this heart aspect of our faith and try to live out our religion solely as correct doctrine or ethics, our passion is crippled, or perverted, and the divorce of our soul from the heart purposes of God toward us is deepened."[7] -John Eldredge, *The Sacred Romance*

Experience

The next element of the philosophy of sport in ministry is experience. Experiencing Christ in life enables me to understand.

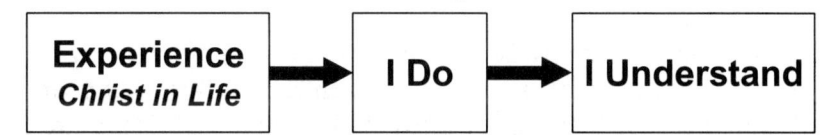

Experience Christ in Life → **I Do** → **I Understand**

An initial part of experiencing the truth of the gospel is through imitation. The Church in Thessalonica imitated Paul, Silas, and Timothy, *"You became imitators of us and of the Lord; in spite of severe suffering, you welcomed the message with the joy given by the Holy Spirit. And so you became a model to all the believers in Macedonia and Achaia."*[8] (italics added) The people of the Church in Thessalonica must have observed that there was something authentic and genuine in Paul, Silas, and Timothy lives'. The truth these men lived, day in and day out, was attractive to them—attractive enough for the Thessalonians to imitate. As they began to imitate and pattern their lives after these men, they began to experience the truth of the gospel in their own lives. This imitation led to the believers' understanding of the reality of the gospel and how it should be carried out in every aspect of life. The authenticity of life in Christ became a reality to the believers in Thessalonica, eventually resulting in a change of allegiance to follow Christ. The people experienced freedom from the burden of sin and the freedom to have a restored relationship with God, with self, others and all of Creation.

Similarly, sportspeople learn through imitation. Years ago in tennis the one-handed backhand was the only backhand technique in tennis. When professionals Jimmy Connors and Chrissy Evert started using a new backhand technique—the two-handed backhand—and won the singles championships at Wimbledon, everyone started imitating them. Even thirty years later people still use the two handed backhand modeled for them by Evert and Connors because it works!

The first person to make famous the dunk in basketball was Dr. J, player for the NBA Philadelphia 76ers. How did others

CHAPTER THREE

learn how to dunk? They saw his example, imitated it and loved the experience of it. As a result, the dunk is now one of the most popular moves in the sport of basketball both for the individual executing it and spectators as well!

When people of sport demonstrate and proclaim the truth of the gospel in sport, as is the case with the imitation of sport techniques, others will be attracted to imitate. This imitation, experiencing the gospel in action, will lead them to understand who Christ is. We must be careful in our modeling that we don't simply model the gospel on Sunday mornings at Church, just in weekly Bible Studies, or merely in prayers said before or after games, but throughout all of life. Our love for Christ must overflow in the way we play, in the way we relate to others, in our conversations, in every detail of our lives. The truth of the gospel is to be experienced and is relevant in all of life. It is vital that people of sport who are believers continue to live among the people of sport to demonstrate and model for them the truth of the gospel in the experience of sport.

> **Our love for Christ must overflow in the way we play, in the way we relate to others, in our conversations, in every detail of our lives.**

"Do not rejoice in this, that the spirits are subject to you, but rather rejoice because your names are written in heaven" (Luke 10:20). "Jesus Christ is saying here, 'Don't rejoice in your successful service for Me, but rejoice because of your right relationship with Me." The trap you may fall into in Christian work is to rejoice in successful service—rejoicing in the fact that God has used you. Yet you will never be able to measure fully what God will do through you if you have a right-standing relationship with Jesus Christ. If you keep your relationship right with Him, then regardless of your circumstances or whoever you encounter each day, He will continue to pour 'rivers of living water' through you (John 7:38). And it is actually by His mercy that He does not let you know it. Once you have the right relationship with God through salvation and sanctification, remember that whatever your circumstances may be, you have been placed in them by God. And God uses the

> reaction of your life to your circumstances to fulfill His purpose as long as you continue to 'walk in the light as He is in the light' (I John 1:7)."[9]
> - Oswald Chambers, *My Utmost for His Highest*

Integration

The fourth element of the philosophy of sport in ministry is integration. Integration involves understanding the "why;" that is, the reason behind the experience in order to appropriately apply it. We are told that the Thessalonians experienced and understood the gospel through the power of the Holy Spirit in their lives so that they, in turn, became a model to others. Their faith was so vibrant and real it was known throughout the Mediterranean region. Instead of simply imitating Paul, Silas, and Timothy, the believers were motivated to apply their faith to all of life through the power of the Holy Spirit. The change of allegiance that happened in their lives restored their relationship with Christ and flowed over into all their relationships. Their restored relationship with Christ removed their old, selfish motivations, replacing them with a Christ-motivated value system! They experienced the reality of Christ in their lives and became a model for living a Christ-filled life by the way they integrated the truth of the gospel in all they did.

It is important to note, however, that integration is more than merely setting up standards of behavior such as "I will not play dirty to gain an unfair advantage," or "I will not swear when I get angry." It is not simply carrying out a behavioral code. Integration happens when I understand the truth of the gospel and wholeheartedly embrace it and apply it to every detail of my life. Simply stated, I understand who I am in Christ, and His presence in my life is displayed in all I do. True integration is "letting the perfect qualities of Jesus exhibit themselves in my human flesh"[10] without my being consciously aware of it. Finally, we have the following as our model of integration for sport in ministry:

> **Integration happens when I understand the truth of the gospel and wholeheartedly embrace it and apply it to every detail of my life.**

Integration *Christ in You* → **I Know Why** → **I Commit**

This means that my commitment is first to my relationship with Christ and then to bringing His presence into all of the activities in my life. This model illustrates how it is possible—through the hearts of sportspeople committed to Christ—that sport can be restored.

> **The context of sport is a laboratory in which the imitation, integration, and emulation of Christ can take place.**

> "The most wonderful secret of living a holy life does not lie in imitating Jesus, but in letting the perfect qualities of Jesus exhibit themselves in my human flesh. Sanctification is 'Christ in you the hope of Glory' (Colossians 1:28). It is his wonderful life that is imparted to me in sanctification—imparted by faith as a sovereign gift of God's grace. Sanctification means the impartation of the holy qualities of Jesus Christ to me. It is the gift of His patience, love, holiness, faith, purity, and godliness that is exhibited in and through every sanctified soul. Sanctification is not drawing from Jesus the power to be holy—it is drawing from Jesus the very holiness that was exhibited in Him, and that He now exhibits in me. Sanctification is an impartation, not an imitation. Imitation is something altogether different. The perfection of everything is in Jesus Christ, and the mystery of sanctification is that all the perfect qualities of Jesus are at my disposal...But of Him you are in Christ Jesus, who became for us...sanctification...-I Corinthians 1:30."[11]
>
> –Oswald Chambers, *My Utmost for His Highest*

The context of sport is a laboratory in which the imitation, integration, and emulation of Christ can take place. When we are involved in competition, it makes us take action-based intellectual, attitudinal, and behavioral choices. We build patterns of behavior and these patterns shape our worldview. Sport is a breeding ground of pressure points that publicize what is in a person's heart.

Typically in ministry we teach principles and try to get people to incorporate them in their lives. But people don't learn how to apply values of life through words and definitions. People learn best through relationships, which is why sport is an effective place to teach values and attitudes. Sportspeople naturally tend to emulate other sportspeople, though often looking at role models without regard to their values. This is why in sport in ministry it is critical to have role models who live out their allegiance to Christ in their lives on and off the playing pitch and courts. These role models will live lives worth of imitation.

> "Young people do not assimilate the values of their group by learning the words and their definition. They learn attitudes, habits and ways of judging. They learn these in intensely personal transactions with their immediate family or associates. They learn them in the routine and the crisis of living, but they also learn them through songs, stories, drama and games. They do not learn ethical principles but they emulate ethical (or unethical) people. They do not analyze or list the attributes they wish to develop; they identify with people who seem to them to have these attributes. That is why young people need models, but in their imaginative life and in their environment they need models of what man at his best can be."
>
> –J.W. Gardner[12]

Philosophy of Sport In Ministry

- Proclamation: Christ in Word
  I Hear - I Forget
- Demonstration: Christ in Action
  I See - I Remember
- Experience: Christ in Life
  I Do - I Understand
- Integration: Christ in You
  I Know Why - I Commit

CHAPTER THREE

In today's culture, as a way of validating truth, people want to see it, taste it, and experience it for themselves. It is through experience that we test whether things are true. In sport in ministry, the sport arena is a valid place for not yet believers to test the truth of the gospel in the crucible of the sport experience. It is also a vital place to proclaim, demonstrate, experience and integrate our commitment to the truth of the Gospel. As we minister to people of sport, we want them to see the Word of God proclaimed, demonstrated, experienced and integrated in our lives. We want to show them and have them test out for themselves that He is God of Truth in word, in deed, and in life. This is why the philosophical foundations of proclamation, demonstration, experience and integration are highly relevant sport in ministry. They provide the model for how the gospel can be lived out to the people of sport. The following chapter introduces the McCown Sport in Ministry Map. This visual perspective will help identify your target audience and to help you think through how best to serve them. It will help you determine how to best live out the gospel to the target group of people of sport you are trying to reach.

> **In sport in ministry, the sport arena is a valid place for not yet believers to test the truth of the gospel in the crucible of the sport experience.**

Questions to think about:

1. What sport concepts or techniques have you learned purely through imitation? Who demonstrated this to you? What attracted you to imitate this person?

2. "Seeing is believing." How does this statement relate to the philosophy of sport in ministry?

3. What are the differences between doing and being? Which precedes the other? Which is more important?

4. How can the activity of sport reflect Christ's glory? What would the sport activity look like?

5. What would it mean to fully integrate Christ in your sport experience? What changes would need to be made?

6. Where in the sport experience itself can we proclaim, demonstrate, experience, and integrate Christ?

A Visual Perspective–
The McCown Sport in Ministry Map

CHAPTER FOUR

God is creating a growing network of diverse ministries in sport throughout the world. In fact, there are well over 100 models of sports ministry to date. In 1998, twenty-four sports ministry leaders representing fourteen countries from six continents of the world met in Bangkok, Thailand, to discuss the development of sports ministry worldwide. As the meeting progressed, there was disagreement and confusion over what sports ministry is. The leaders believed what they were doing in their respective ministries was the most effective way to do sports ministry. In an effort to explain the diverse perspectives, it was during this meeting that Lowrie McCown began drawing a diagram to encompass all the different ministries represented. This diagram is now known as the McCown Sport in Ministry Map. Birthed out of a desire to bring a visual, universal perspective to sports ministry, the Sport in Ministry Map is a tool that can chart every ministry that seeks to incorporate sports ministry. It depicts the vast breadth and depth of the terrain of sports ministry. Within that terrain, you can identify the location of your own sports ministry. Like any good map, it enables you to know where you are and helps you know how to get to where you want to be. The map serves as an alignment tool providing landmarks allowing you to set boundaries for your ministries. In this way, the landmarks will help ensure that you keep your focus on your target audience.

People involved in sports ministry prefer a pragmatic approach to ministry. We see or hear of an effective sports ministry program and try to implement it in our own situation, oftentimes without regard to the cultural, environmental, or population differences between our target group and that of the model. We neglect to take into account that what works in one situation may not work equally well in others. Instead of blindly following someone else's lead, with the help of the Sport in Ministry Map, your ministry group can tailor your ministry to best meet the needs of the particular people of sport in your area.

What is unique about the Sport in Ministry Map is that it encompasses the whole panorama of sports: individual sports, team sports, adventure camping, outdoor survival training, orienteering and extreme sports. Likewise, it includes all people of sport: participants, trainers (coaches), managers, administrators, agents, parents of participants, and sport support professionals. Lastly, the Map is free from cultural, age or gender bias, and it is not chronological, which further illustrates its broad use.

The Sport in Ministry Map is comprised of two axes: the sport experience continuum and the spiritual continuum. The horizontal or sport experience continuum, developed by Lowrie, outlines where people are, according to their experience in sport. The vertical, or spiritual continuum, is taken from the Engel Scale[1] developed by James Engel in the 1970's to show the process of evangelism and discipleship. It outlines where people are in relationship to Christ. Further, it demonstrates the process of how people come to Christ (evangelism) and where people are in relationship to Christ (discipleship). The Sport in Ministry Map shows where you are on the Map and gives you a way to systematically diagram people to whom you want to minister. Using these axes, we can identify target audiences for sport in ministry in terms of their position along the horizontal and vertical continuums. That is, we can map where our target populations are in terms of both their sport and the spiritual experiences. In the following pages, we will first discuss the sport experience continuum and its implications for ministry, and then the spiritual continuum and its implications for ministry.

Spiritual Experience

Experience

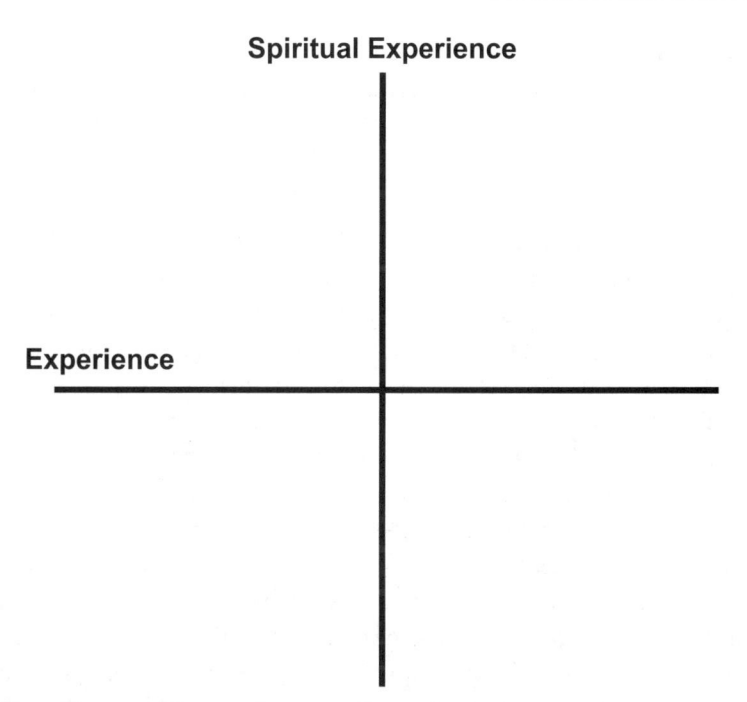

The Sport Experience Continuum
– the horizontal axis

The horizontal axis on the Sport in Ministry Map represents the sport experience continuum. This continuum describes the complete range of people who have an interest in or participate in sport. It is important to note that this continuum refers to the *mindset* that people bring to their sport experience. It is their *perspective* of sport, not simply their abilities in sport that determines where they are on the sport experience continuum.

At the far left of the continuum are the Spectators. Spectators are people who love to watch competitive sport events. Spectators are also called "fans" because they are *fanatical*, super enthusiastic, about sports. They are media-driven—they watch sports on television, listen to sports radio, read sport magazines and the sports pages of the newspapers. These are the people who make the Sports page the most widely read section of the newspaper. Thanks to their interest in sports, there are worldwide satellite, 24-hour a day television and radio "sports-only" broadcasts.

> It is important to note that this continuum refers to the mindset that people bring to their sport experience. It is their perspective of sport, not simply their abilities in sport that determines where they are on the sport experience continuum.

Spectator

The Spectator

Spectators are vicariously involved in sport. In other words, these are the people that live through others' sport experience. Take, for instance, a commentary written about Spectators called The Fan: "Once a week, the fan flees his house and goes to the stadium. Banners wave and the air resounds with noisemakers, firecrackers and drums, it rains streamers and confetti. The city disappears, its routine forgotten; all that exists is the temple. In the sacred place, the only religion without atheists puts its divinities on display; although the fan can contemplate the miracle more comfortably on TV, he prefers to make the pilgrimage to this spot where he can see his angels in the flesh doing battle with the demons of the day. Here the fan shakes his handkerchief, gulps his saliva, swallows his bile, eats his cap, whispers prayers and curses and suddenly breaks out in an ovation, leaping like a flea to hug the stranger at his side cheering the goal. While the pagan mass lasts, the fan is many. Along with thousands of other devotees he shares the certainty that we are the best, that all referees are crooked, that all the adversaries cheat. Rarely does the fan say, 'My club plays today.' Rather he says, 'We play today.' He knows it's 'player number twelve' who stirs up the winds of fervor that propel the ball when she falls asleep, just as the other eleven players know that playing without their fans is like dancing without music. When the game is over, the fan, who has not moved from the stands, celebrates *his* victory: 'What a goal we scored.' 'What a beating we gave them.' Or he cries over his defeat: 'They swindled us again.' 'Thief of a referee.' And then the sun goes down and so does the fan. Shadows fall over the emptying stadium. On the concrete terracing, a few fleeting bonfires burn while the lights and voices fade. The stadium is left alone and the fan, too, returns to his solitude: to the I who had been we. The fan goes off: the crowd breaks up and melts away; and Sunday becomes as melancholy as Ash Wednesday after the death of carnival."[2]

Why do people, like this fan, become so devoted to sports? Why is it that Spectators pay homage and allegiance to their favorite teams? One reason is that people desire to be affiliated with something bigger than they are. People are also attracted to the excellence at which players execute skills and want to know how to do it. People also watch sports because it is an escape from reality. Sports draw them out of their everyday existence and provide relief from daily life. Some Spectators carry their team affiliation too far. In 1994 FIFA World Cup Championship, a defender for the team from Colombia accidentally kicked the ball into his own net during the match against the United States. Colombia went on to lose the match 2-1 and was eliminated in the first round of the tournament. Three days after this player returned home from the World Cup he was shot coming out of a restaurant by an irate Spectator.

Clearly, Spectators represent the largest group we have the opportunity to minister to. As Bud Wilkinson, an American football coach at Oklahoma University in the 1950's said, "A football game is 80,000 people desperately in need of exercise, watching 22 people desperately in need of rest!" Currently there are ministries that reach Spectators at major sporting events by distributing videos to be played at half time, by handing out literature, and by inviting High Profile players to give their testimonies.

> **People desire to be affiliated with something bigger than they are.**

"The rugby fan is, without doubt, a splendid human being. Week after week he'll dig into his wallet and shell out money, which would be more wisely invested...for the dubious privilege of watching the on-field antics of the team to which he has pledged his loyalty. In doing so he harms his budget, his blood pressure and his peace of mind, but these are sacrifices that matter little to the incurable rugby addict. He gets very little in return. He is, by and large, ignored by players, administrators, the referee, the touch judges, the pre-match dancing girls and the fellow selling orange-flavored cold drinks at the main entrance.[3]"
—Andre' Oosthuizen, *They Once Had Horns*

Spectator

|————+————————————————
       Novice

The Novice

The Novice is the second category on the sport experience continuum, just to the right of the Spectator. New to their games, Novices are those participants who are developing sport skills at an introductory or developmental level. Though they have little or no experience in their games, they are actively learning to improve their performance. A 35-year old picking up golf for the first time or a 6-year old playing soccer for the first time are both Novices. Given the desire of Novices to improve basic skills in their sport of interest, effective ministry to this group must include activities that help them achieve this goal. A program that offers good instruction in basic skills, practice in executing individual skills without pressure, and good coaching during competition against other Novices would fit well with the needs of the Novice.

The Leisure

> For the Leisure, sport is a hobby that they enjoy, yet not something they take too seriously.

The third category is Leisure, comprised of people who compete for fun. Their sport is a *hobby* that they enjoy; yet not something they take too seriously. For them, participation is more important than performance results. This does not mean that they are not competitive—they do enjoy winning—but they are not dependent on the results nor overly concerned about their performance. They play simply because they love their sport. After the Spectator, the Leisure category is one of the largest groups of participants. Particularly within the church sport ministry model, the Leisure sport participant is the most common participant.

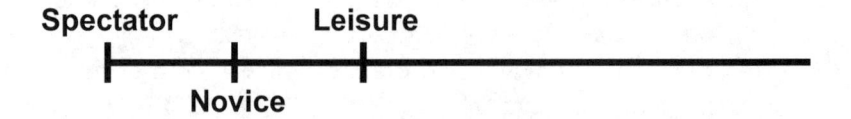

Spectator   **Leisure**
|————+————————|——————————————
       Novice

> Leisure vs. Player "The athlete (player) by definition attempts to excel (perform), to win the contest, but he does not attempt to win an ultimate, cosmic victory because he knows he cannot be God. The casual sportsman (leisure), on the other hand, is not satisfied with spontaneous or undirected play. He does compete in the game in a less skillful and more relaxed way that the athlete (player), but he plays with the knowledge that in playing the game to the best of his ability he can experience a measure of victory."[4]

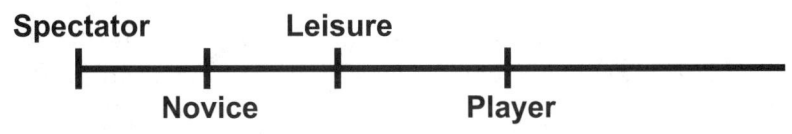

```
Spectator        Leisure
    |---------|---------|---------|
         Novice          Player
```

The Player

Moving to the right half of the sport experience continuum, characteristics of people of sport change significantly. People on this side of the continuum find their *identity* in their sport experience. The first category on this side of the continuum is the Player. Players share a common worldview: they view their lives in relationship to their sport. Their sport defines their lives and they define themselves by their sport. If you ask a Player to tell you a bit about himself, he will reply, "I'm a cricketer" or "I'm a swimmer," or identify himself through whatever sport he plays.

> **Players share a common worldview: they view their lives in relationship to their sport. Their sport defines their lives and they define themselves by their sport.**

Players also know who other Players are. Lowrie followed his 15-year old son's basketball team all year and had identified 7 of the 15 kids on the team to be Players. He asked his son, "Who are the Players on your team?" His son rattled off the names of the same seven Players Lowrie had noticed. Simply being on the team does not make someone a Player. What is interesting is that the members on the team, who are Leisure, likewise know that they are not Players.

Players are known by others on their team and in their community because of their sport. Their successes, achievements, and notoriety all come through their sports performance. Sport can improve one's image but can also destroy one's self-image. A player's self-image is based on the way she performs. If she performs well her self-image is good, if she plays poorly her self-image suffers. Self-image is a huge ministry issue. Players that come to Christ need to find their identity in Christ rather than in sport. If this does not take place, Players try to perform for Christ in the same way they performed to have a healthy self-image before they came to Christ. Sport ministries directed to Players who already know Christ need to help them realize that their identity is in Christ alone and not in their performance. Players are willing to take the risk to find a healthy self-image.

What sets the Players on a team apart is the fact that they are highly competitive and extremely motivated by their performance. Unlike Leisure, they are concerned with performance as much as or more than winning. They are internally driven to be the best, seeking internal perfection. They are willing to sacrifice a great deal for the ability to perform at their best level. Focused on their personal ability level, discipline and training become their highest priority. They constantly compare themselves against other Players they play and compete with. Though they evaluate themselves continually, they rarely talk to teammates about assessment of themselves and the related issues of the fear of failure. Typically, they think they are the only ones dealing with such heart issues that develop from this performance pressure.

Even off the court or playing field, Players' lifestyles and experiences are affected by their sport. Every area of their lives is affected by the drive to perform at the top level. Most of their experiences are sports-related (for example, Players choose to be conscious of nutritional choices and dedicate many hours of their day to training demands and practice), and all of their life experiences are filtered and processed through their sport experience.

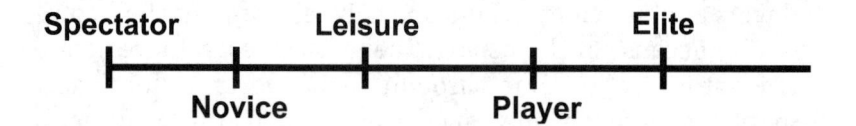

> **What sets the Players on a team sport is the fact that they are highly competitive and extremely motivated by their performance.**

Spectator — Novice — Leisure — Player — Elite

The Elite

The Elite in sport possesses all the characteristics of the Player coupled with a greater fear of failure. Despite their fear of failure, however, they are still willing to play, risking failure for the opportunity to succeed. Elite players have increasingly more to lose as they play the game. They have a deeper understanding of sacrifice to reach goals. Even more so than the Players, they are concerned with individual performance over winning and losing.

The Elite risk their health every time they go out on the court or field. Jim Otto, Hall of Famer in the National Football (American football) league sustained the following injuries and subsequent surgeries during his career in order to keep on playing: 18 knee surgeries, 2 knee replacements, 32 broken noses, 150 stitches on his face, 30 concussions, and 1 back surgery.[5]

Psychological well-being is key to the Elite player's sports performance. An Elite player must be able to maintain emotional stability to achieve maximum performance. Despite playing under prolonged conditions of uncertainty and stress, they must control their emotions. When the Elite denies their fear, they commit to a level of individual bravery and self-sacrifice for the sake of the team.

With so much at stake, Elite players often become ritualistic and superstitious in their behaviors. They have to put on their socks and shoes a certain way, wear a lucky necklace, sit in a certain seat on the bus, eat a certain food for a pre-game meal, or wear a special glove. The British Soccer team was so superstitious that they hired a witch to help their team in prepare for the 1994 European Cup competition. Patrick Roy, who played 18 seasons with the Canadiens and Avalanche hockey teams as one of Canada's best and most scientific goalies, was so superstitious that he would never step on lines. Such rituals and superstitions emerge to help the Elite Player stay in control to handle the moods and motivations that crop up in this high-stress environment.

> **Elite players have increasingly more to lose as they play the game. They have a deeper understanding of sacrifice to reach goals.**

In addition to behavior patterns, many social complexities also arise when someone reaches the level of an Elite player. Relational and role ambiguities are accentuated by risk. That is, the judgments Elite players make are often compromised by their all-consuming view of their sport as the first priority in their lives.

> "He's the envy of the neighborhood: the one who escaped the factory or the office and gets paid to have fun. He won the lottery. And even if he does have to sweat buckets, with no right to fatigue or failure, he gets into the papers and on TV, his name is on the radio, women swoon over him and children yearn to be like him. He started out playing for pleasure in the dirt streets of the slums, and now he plays out of duty in stadiums where he has no choice but to win. Businessmen buy him, sell him, lend him; and he lets it all happen in return for the promise of more fame and more money. The more successful he is and the more money he makes, the more of a prisoner he becomes: forced into military discipline, he suffers the punishing daily round of training and the bombardments of painkillers and cortisone to forget his aches and fool his body; and on the eve of the big games, they lock him up in a concentration camp where he does forced labor, eats tasteless food, gets drunk on water and sleeps alone. In other human trades, decline comes with old age, but a player can be old at thirty. Muscles tire early: 'That guy couldn't score if the field were on a slope.' Not even if they tied the goalie's hands." Or before thirty if the ball knocks him out badly, or bad luck tears a muscle, or a kick breaks a bone so it can't be."[6]
> –Eduardo Galeano, *Soccer in the Sun and Shadow*

The Elite compete against their own teammates for playing time and/or positions, even though they realize at some level that cooperation with teammates is imperative to ensure victory. This tension creates a strange dissonance between cooperation and competition, especially when the team oftentimes is their only constant and reliable source of social interaction. For many reasons, it is difficult for Elite to know who their real friends are. Though they are well known in their community and in nearby communities as well, it is hard to discern whether the motivations of the people who want to be their friends are genuine or for selfish gains. In the case of club and high performance players, the constant threat of trade makes it difficult to form stable social relationships outside of the team. So, despite the fact that their teammates often fulfill their need for friendship, Elite players are so competitive that they place their own performance, and by extension, their own interests, above those of their team and teammates.

The Elite are pampered because of the celebrity status that they have attained and they are often viewed as entertainers. Their every move is observed and commented on publicly. Constantly being in the spotlight contributes to the tremendous pressure that the Elite player feels. There is also the risk of injury that can end a career in the blink of an eye. Needless to say, the pressure to succeed is great, with just a small window of time to make this happen.

> "One of the perks of becoming a successful athlete is being in the public eye. One of the drawbacks faced by the successful athlete is being in the public eye. The public doesn't allow the athlete to be ordinary. Being an athlete means that in some way you're different, that you have physical ability or drive that is beyond others...that single extraordinary trait can be magnified under the public microscope until it permeates every area of your life. You are expected to do more than just perform well. You're expected to win, both on the playing field and in other aspects of your life. If you don't the public can quickly turn on you."[7]
> -George Selleck, *How to Play the Game of Your Life*

```
Spectator        Leisure           Elite
   |----|----------|----------|---------|----|
       Novice              Player        High Profile
```

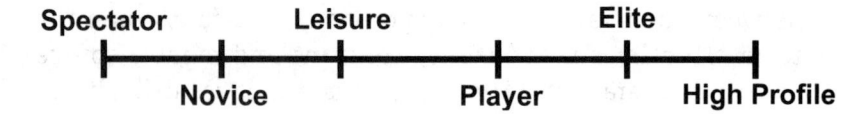

The High Profile

To the far right of the sport experience continuum are the High Profile players. These are the Michael Jordans and David Beckhams of sport. High Profile players have all the Player and Elite characteristics plus a few more arising from their fame and popularity. Based on the celebrity they have achieved, they face idolatry by fans, which results in an extreme loss of privacy for them. For example, when Michael Jordan goes to church, he has to sign autographs while the Pastor is preaching. He can't even sit in church without having his privacy violated!

> ### the idol
>
> "...He is born in a straw crib in a tin-roofed shack and he enters the world clinging to a ball.
>
> From the moment he learns to walk, he knows how to play. In his early years he brings joy to the sandlots, plays like crazy in the back alleys of the slums until night falls and you can't see the ball, and in his early manhood he takes flight and the stadiums fly with him. His acrobatic art draws multitudes, Sunday after Sunday from victory to victory ovation to ovation.
>
> The ball seeks him out, knows him, needs him. She rests and rocks on the top of his foot. He caresses her and makes her speak, and in that tete-a-tete millions of mutes converse. The nobodies, those condemned to always be nobodies, feel they are somebodies for a moment by virtue of those one- two passes, those dribbles that draw Z's on the grass, those incredible backheel goals or overhead volleys. When he plays, the team has twelve players: "Twelve? It has fifteen! Twenty!"
>
> The ball laughs, radiant, in the air. He brings her down, puts her to sleep, showers her with compliments, dances with her, and seeing such things never before seen his admirers pity their unborn grandchildren who will never see them.

> But the idol is an idol for only a moment, a human eternity, all of nothing; and when the time comes for the golden foot to become a lame duck, the star will have completed his journey from sparkle to blackout. His body has more patches than a clown's suit, and by now the acrobat is a cripple, the artist a beast of burden: 'Not with your clodhoppers!'
>
> The fountain of public adulation becomes the lightning rod of public rancor: 'You mummy!' Sometimes the idol doesn't fall all at once. And sometimes when he breaks, people devour the pieces."[8]
> —Eduardo Galeano, *Soccer in the Sun and Shadow*

Like Elite, High Profile players have a tendency to be spoiled. Because of their elevated status in society there is a feeling that High Profile are exempt from the basic rules of society and culture. We create this permissive environment for them by making excuses for their misbehavior. Do you remember when Maradona had a drug problem? Did the fans ever ostracize him for that? No, they excused him, saying, "He had to release stress somehow." They seemed to believe that such behavior was okay because he was Maradona!

High Profile players put their sport performance above all else. This was the case with New Zealand Maori team member Jonah Lomu, the highest paid rugby player in the world. Despite awaiting a kidney transplant and discouragement from his medical doctors against competing, Lomu stated, "I'd put everything on the line to play in the World Cup…my dream is to play in a World Cup and win a World Cup. That would complete my life story."[9]

> **High Profile players put their sport performance above all else.**

> "It's obvious, folks, that our lives are parallel to yours-the-joys of success, the agony of defeat-the difference is we live our lives out on the public stage, often with unqualified and unauthorized judges deciding whether the job is done well or not. We have high profiles and live in glass houses, but we laugh, we cry and worry the same as you do."[10]
> –John Lucas, former NBA player

> "Because you're in the public eye, people are always gushing over you, telling you how great you are and all that mushy malarkey. They want my autograph! For what? Maybe I'm a jerk, maybe I'm a heel. How do they know? They just see me play basketball."[11]
> -Dave Cowens, NBA Hall of Fame player

Remember that the Sport in Ministry Map is not chronological or age-biased. This means that it is possible to have a young person who is a High Profile player. Take, for example, Joey, a 14-year-old High Profile player playing soccer on a high performance soccer club. Everyone knows him by his first name because he is the best in the club. And even though he plays for a team that is based five hours away from where Lowrie's son plays, no matter where you are in the state of Georgia, if you are talking youth soccer and mention the name "Joey," everyone knows exactly whom you are talking about!

There are very few recognizable names per sport, per community, per city, per country, or worldwide. The "Joeys" of the world are indeed the exceptions. There are even fewer High Profile players who are Christians. When sports ministries need a speaker we all want to invite a High Profile player.

To summarize the right side of the sport experience continuum, here is a quote spoken from the heart of a basketball Player, "You begin by bouncing the ball-in the house, on the driveway, along the sidewalk, at the playground. Then you start shooting: legs bent, eyes on the rim, elbow under the ball. You shoot and follow through. Let it fly, up, up and in. No

---

There are very few recognizable names per sport, per community, per city, per country, or worldwide... There are even fewer High Profile players who are Christians.

equipment is needed beyond a ball, a rim and imagination. How simple the basic act is. I'm not sure exactly when my interest turned to passion but I was very young, and it never diminished. When I was a teenager, alone in the gym for hours, the repetition of shooting, shot after shot, became a kind of ritual to me. The seams and the grain of the leather ball had to feel a certain way. My fingertips went right to the grooves and told me if it felt right. The key to the fingertips was keeping them clean. I would rub my hand to my sweaty brow, then against my t-shirt at chest level, and then I would cradle the ball. By the end of shooting practice, the grime had made it's way from the floor to the ball to my fingertips to my shirt. After thousands of shots, my shirts were permanently stained."[12] If you process life through your sport experience like this, you are on the right side of the Sport in Ministry Map!

The Spiritual Continuum– the vertical axis

Ted Ward, retired professor at Trinity International Seminary, was speaking at a conference in West Africa. During his talk he used the terms "non-believers" and "believers." Each time he used the word "non-believer," puzzled looks came over the audience members' faces. When he was finished speaking he asked, "Why was everyone looking at me like that?" They asked him, "What is a non-believer? We don't have any here." He said, "What do you mean, everyone here is a Christian?" "Oh, no," they answered. Ted rebutted, "So you do have non-believers." "No, sir, we don't." Exasperated Ted asked, "Well, what do you have?" They announced, "Not yet believers."

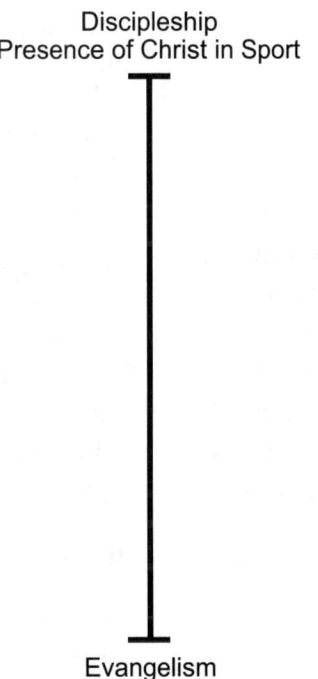

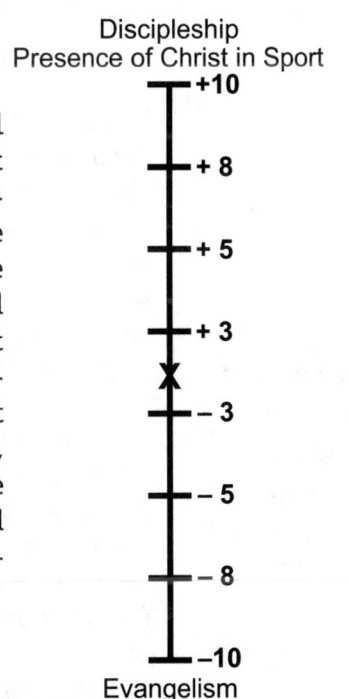

The West Africans perceived that people are eventually going to come to Christ, they just haven't yet. They truly viewed all people as being on a continuum of spirituality. Such a perspective reminds us that we are all on a journey and that God has placed us in peoples' lives to be a part of their journey toward Christ as well.

In the Sport in Ministry Map, the lower portion of the spiritual continuum, labeled "Evangelism-Presenting Christ through Sports," represents how people come to Christ. To use the West Africans' terms, these are the "not yet believers." The "believers" are located in the top portion of the continuum, labeled "Discipleship-the Presence of Christ in Sport." In our sport valued context, discipleship is the process of training believing people in sport to become more like Christ in their sport activities and all other areas of life.

> **In our sport valued context, discipleship is the process of training believing people in sport to become more like Christ in their sport activities and all other areas of life.**

How do we do evangelism through sport? Typically, we present a sport analogy or sport story that teaches a biblical principle. For example, the apostle Paul uses sport analogies such as "run in such a way as to gain the prize,"[13] to illustrate how resolved one should be in following Christ.

In contrast to evangelism, however, when you start to do discipleship, the analogies and stories have less impact on the sportsperson. It is the integration of Scripture in their lives that will guide believers' conduct in the sport experience. Scripture is vitally relevant to each individual's sport experience and activity, and it is the application of Scripture to their sport experience that enables them to grow in Christlikeness through these activities.

> **It is the integration of Scripture in their lives that will guide believers' conduct in the sport experience.**

The numbers alongside the Engel Scale, spiritual continuum represent where someone is in the process of growing towards Christlikeness. The lower half of the continuum represents the process of bringing someone to Christ. A "–10" refers to someone who has no awareness of God, no idea at all of who God is. Progressing up the continuum, a "–5" refers to someone with a basic knowledge of the gospel. Perhaps this person would know the stories of Jesus' birth, death, and resurrection, though there is no personal identification to the story

Discipleship
Presence of Christ in Sport

```
              +10   Christ likeness

              + 8

"In" Christ

              + 5   Spiritual Reproduction

              + 3   Incorporated into the Church
               X    Change of Allegiance
              − 3   Sin Recognition

"To" Christ
              − 5   Gospel Basics

              − 8

              −10   No Belief in God
```

Evangelism
Presenting Christ Through Sports

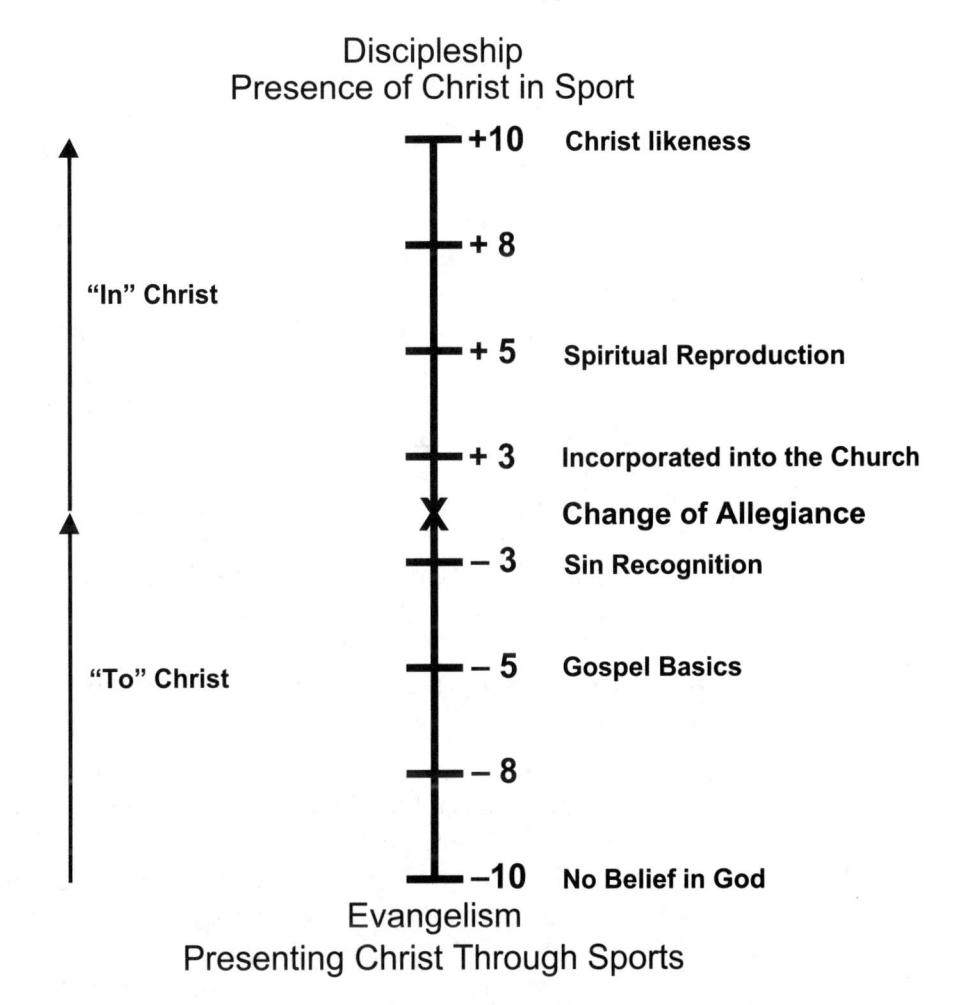

or relevance to his life. A person described by a "−3" has a positive attitude toward Christ, but as yet has made no commitment to follow Him. Further up on the axis, someone who recognizes the problem of sin in his life, his need for repentance, the available forgiveness through Christ and is close to the point of a change of allegiance, is marked by an "X" on the scale. An individual at the "X" acknowledges that Christ is the way to Life and makes a radical change of allegiance from living for himself to living for Christ. This is the midpoint of the continuum.

The upper half of the continuum represents discipleship—the transformation process of growing in Christ and becoming more like Christ. Growing in Christ requires that a believer undergo a re-evaluation process, developing a Christlike perspective in the way he relates to issues such sexuality, drugs, relationships and sport. Progressing up the continuum, "+3" denotes someone who is active in a church, not merely attending services, but becoming involved in the ministries of a local church. A "+5" refers to a person who is engaged in "spiritual reproduction," exhibiting and sharing the love of Christ with others, which leads them to grow towards Christ. A "+10" represents Christlikeness, a goal to which we all should aspire; yet none of us will reach in this lifetime.

To summarize, then, sport in ministry on the lower half of the continuum helps people to grow closer to a change of allegiance. Sport in ministry on the upper half of the continuum enables people to grow in Christ.

Implications of spiritual continuum for sport in ministry

Evangelism entails sowing and watering spiritual seeds. It takes a long time for a seed to grow. A farmer cannot see the harvest without first going through the process of tilling the soil, planting the seed, and nurturing the plant. The Billy Graham Evangelistic Association says that it takes seven separate encounters with the gospel before someone is ready to make a decision for Christ. This is not to say that Christ cannot take someone immediately to the point of conversion. Rather, the point is that He typically leads people through a process of coming to Him.

> "The model of a pilgrimage, or journey, envisions conversions differently. Once an initial response to the gospel has taken place, the pilgrim joins other believers as they walk down that narrow way of death to self and new life in Christ. All that is asked of the pilgrim is a desire to know the reality of these life changing truths...Conviction of sin leads to receiving forgiveness and rebirth through Jesus. And when spiritual

> regeneration has taken place, the pilgrim hopefully will persevere and grow in grace through spiritual sanctification. The process of becoming a disciple is never completed in this life. Conversions is just one, albeit essential stage in the process, but it is not in and of itself the goal."[14]
> —James Engel and William A Dyrness, *Changing the Mind of Missions*

The vast majority of sports ministry groups today, however, do not see evangelism as a process. They instead focus on the middle portion of the continuum, with particular emphasis on the point of conversion. But if the focus is solely on that single point of conversion, the "X," we may not fully see what we are doing as effective ministry. In practice, we evaluate ministries based on the number of conversions, the number of people who have come to Christ. We believe that if attendees at a sport camp have walked an aisle, prayed a prayer to accept Jesus, or raised a hand, we can now determine whether they have made a commitment to Christ. Our typical standard of evaluation is based on numbers and logic. Of course, it is much easier to measure someone reaching the point of conversion than it is to measure someone moving up from a "–5" to a "–3" on the continuum. Nevertheless, it is very possible to have an effective ministry that may never see people come to Christ at the "X" point yet is still helping them journey to "–10" to a "–8" or from a "–5" to a "–3".

For example, there is a story of a missionary in the South Sea Islands who ministered for 28 years but did not see one person convert during his lifetime. Yet at his funeral over 1000 people came to know Christ. Ministry should not be determined by our need to communicate the message, but rather should be based on the needs of the people to whom we are ministering and their unique position on the spiritual continuum. The goal should be helping people in the process of growing to and in Christ. Often we call people to a commitment to Christ when they might not be ready. They may be at a "–5" or "–3" on the spiritual continuum, but because we put our need to see their conversion before their

> The vast majority of sports ministry groups today, do not see evangelism as a process. They instead focus on the middle portion of the continuum with particular emphasis on the point of conversion.

need for a change of allegiance to Christ—we are left to wonder why they aren't growing in their faith!

If you add up all the numbers of converts published by evangelical mission associations, the world has been saved $2\frac{1}{2}$ times over the years. Clearly, these figures show we have not focused on helping people grow in Christ. The mission strategy in the past has been to evangelize the whole world, but this is not what Matthew 28:16 says. It directs us to "make disciples." Evangelism, "-10" to "X" and discipleship, "X" to "+10" are both equally necessary parts of the ultimate goal of striving towards Christlikeness. Approaching Christlikeness is a life long journey. Those of us who know Christ are being sanctified everyday to a higher level of commitment to and knowledge of Christ. Those who do not know Christ may journey from an unawareness of God, to a basic knowledge of the gospel, to an understanding of gospel implications and a change of allegiance, re-evaluation, sanctification, and spiritual reproduction.

This being the case, we cannot focus all of our efforts on evangelism to the exclusion of discipleship. Matthew 28:16-20 says, "Then the eleven disciples went to Galilee, to the mountain where Jesus had told them to go. When they saw him, they worshipped him; but some doubted. Then Jesus came to them and said, 'All authority in heaven and on earth has been given to me. Therefore go and *make disciples* of all nations, baptizing them in the name of the Father and of the Son and of the Holy Spirit, and teaching them to obey everything I have commanded you. And surely I am with you always, to the very end of the age.'" Our age, however, has interpreted Christ's commandment to read that we must go and *evangelize* the world. But that's not what Christ says. He tells us to "Go, and make disciples..." The Greek translation of this passage says, "Going, therefore, make disciples of all nations, baptizing them in the name of the Father, Son and Holy Spirit teaching them to observe all I have commanded you." The "go" actually means going. As we are going through life we are to make disciples. The emphasis of the command is not on the "go" but on the "making disciples".

> **Approaching Christlikeness is a life long journey.**

> **As we are going through life we to make disciples. The emphasis of the command is not on the "go" but on the making of disciples.**

McCown Sport in Ministry Map - Engel's Scale
Discipleship - "Presence of Christ in Sport"

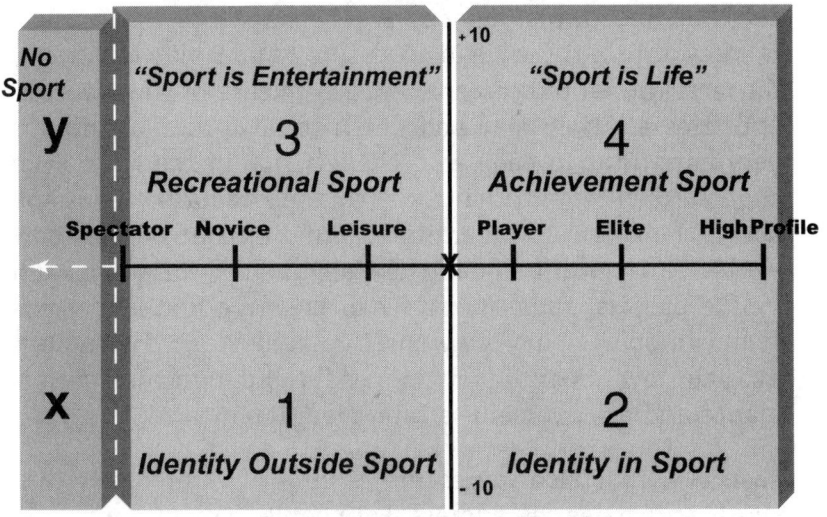

	"Sport is Entertainment"	"Sport is Life"
No Sport	3 Recreational Sport	4 Achievement Sport
	Spectator Novice Leisure	Player Elite High Profile
	1 Identity Outside Sport	2 Identity in Sport

+10 / -10

Evangelism - "Presenting Christ through Sport"

The Engel Scale, the spiritual continuum, is an illustration of the journey of coming to Christ and growing in Him. Our task for sport in ministry is to help people grow in their understanding of Christ wherever they are on the spiritual continuum. When we think of sport in ministry we must have in our minds more than just evangelism. The authors propose that ministry to people on all parts of the spiritual continuum should be equally valued.

Four quadrants of the Sport in Ministry Map

The two axes divide the Sport in Ministry Map into four quadrants. Quadrant 1, the lower left quadrant, represents people whose identity is found outside of sport and who are not yet believers. Quadrant 2, on the lower right hand, represents Players who find their identity in sport and are not yet believers. Quadrant 3, the upper left-hand side are people who know Christ and are involved in sport for leisure and recreational purposes but do not derive their identity from sport. Quadrant 4, the upper right corner, represents people who know Christ and are highly competitive. Numbering the quadrants simply provides reference points for discussion.

The quadrants represent the mindset that people have toward their sport experience. For people on the left side of the Map, Spectators, Novices, and Leisure participants sport is entertainment. People in quadrants 1 and 3 play for strictly for recreational purposes. Sport is a release of life's worries and stresses. They play and watch to have fun. Winning is very important to people on the left side of the Map. Even though they would identify with their favorite team and sport, their personal identity is found outside of the sport world. On the right side of the Map, Players, Elite and High Profile players, sport is life. Their meaning and identity is found in sport. They play sport to achieve at the highest possible level. Winning is important but personal performance and achievement is even more important.

> **Each quadrant represents a unique set of needs that sports ministries can address.**

Each quadrant also represents a unique set of needs that sports ministries can address. For people in quadrants 1 and 3 they are interested in faith stories of Elite and High Profile players and sport stories. Ministries targeting people in quadrants 1 and 3 are program driven usually featuring an entertainment appeal of a High Profile player or a sport demonstration to draw a big crowd. Ministry to quadrants 2 and 4 are relationship driven. Because of the ambiguity of not knowing who their friends are effective ministry involves developing trusting relationships. Players, Elite and High Profile are interested in how to improve in their sport and are interested in sharing their sport experience stories. Successful ministry to people on the right side of the Map entails valuing sport and the sport experience.

The authors realize that not everyone is interested in sport. People who do not have a mindset for sport are noted by "x" and "y" to the left of the Map. People who do not know Christ yet are represented by "x" and "y" are believers who have no interest in sport.

Principles of Partnership in Ministry

In John 11, the story of Jesus raising Lazarus from the dead, we are given a beautiful illustration of the awesome partnership that God enables us to share with Him in the process of evangelism and discipleship. This partnership has specific roles and responsibilities for each partner. The story of Lazarus' physical death to physical life parallels the process of someone going from spiritual death to spiritual life.

Jesus' beloved friend Lazarus was dying in Bethany. Lazarus' sisters, Mary and Martha, send word to Jesus that they need Him to come and heal their brother. After hearing the news, Jesus replied, "This sickness will not end in death. No, it is for God's glory so that God's Son may be glorified through it."[15] Jesus stayed for two more days in Jerusalem. Why didn't Jesus hurry to Bethany to heal Lazarus? Because the fundamental purpose of ministry is that God is glorified. Why does Jesus seemingly wait and not hustle to bring people to the point of conversion today? So that God will be *glorified*. It is Jesus' prerogative and task in ministry to bring glory Himself.

When Mary and Martha send word to Jesus that they need Jesus to heal their brother, they *intercede* on behalf of their brother Lazarus to the One who could meet their needs. Our first responsibility in the evangelism process is to intercede to Jesus on behalf of people who are spiritually dead. This is our privilege and task. We are to tell Jesus their needs and plead on their behalf to the One who can bring them from spiritual death to spiritual life.

When Jesus decides to go to Bethany He tells the disciples, "Lazarus is dead, and for your sake I am glad I was not there, so that you may believe."[16] Significantly for us, Jesus knows what has to occur in order for us to believe. When Martha hears that Jesus is on His way, she goes out to meet Him alone, telling Jesus the bottom line: "Lord, if you had been here, my brother would not have died. But I know even now God will give you whatever you ask."[17] What faith Martha had in Jesus! Jesus responds to Martha with His bottom line, "I am the resurrection and the life. He who believes in me will live, even though he dies; and whoever lives and believes in me will never die. Do you believe that?"[18] This story was not simply about physical death and physical life; Jesus tells her the way to eternal spiritual life, through belief in Himself.

CHAPTER FOUR

Martha goes back to the house and tells Mary that Jesus is about to enter the village. Mary runs to meet him and everyone at the house follows her. When Mary sees Jesus, she falls at his feet and weeps. What is Jesus' response? He weeps with her.

Quite simply, Jesus models for us how to responds to people's needs. He responds to Martha in a way that meets her needs by having a theological discussion with her. He responds very differently to Mary to meet her needs. His focus was on the people to whom He is ministering, not on His own needs.

> **Jesus models for us how to respond to people's needs...His focus was on the people to whom He is ministering, not on His own needs.**

When Jesus arrives at Lazarus' tomb He told the people to "Take away the stone." Why did He ask people to roll away the stone when He could have used supernatural power to move the stone? Do you remember the two women that were on the way to Jesus' tomb to anoint his body with spices? We were told that while they were on their way, they asked each other, "Who would roll the stone away from the entrance of the tomb?"[19] "But when they looked up, they saw that the stone, which was very large, had been rolled away."[20] In the Gospel of Matthew we are told that "There was a violent earthquake, for an angel of the Lord came down from heaven and going to the tomb, rolled back the stone and sat on it."[21] Evidently, Jesus is quite capable of moving stones Himself! He does not need help, yet He asks the people around Lazarus' tomb to roll the stone away. By doing so, they may have a part in what God is going to do. Rolling the stone away themselves allows them the opportunity to actively participate in glorifying God.

The stone itself symbolizes hindrances that prevent people from coming to Jesus. The second responsibility we have in ministry is *to roll away these hindrances* so that people can come to Christ. By helping remove hindrances, we participate in God's being glorified as people come to Christ.

> **By helping remove hindrances, we participate in God's being glorified as people come to Christ.**

How are we to roll away stones? Based on this passage, we move stones based on the needs of the person to whom we are ministering, not based on our own needs. We note that Martha is quick to mention that the odor from the tomb will have a terrible stench because Lazarus' body had already been there for four days. Rolling stones is not glamorous work. On the contrary, it is hard work. If the people who were told to move the stone from Lazarus' tomb thought of their own needs, they would not have moved the stone because of the terrible odor. Yet based on Lazarus' need to hear Jesus' voice and to walk out of the tomb, the stone needed to be moved.

"Jesus called in a loud voice, 'Lazarus, come out!' The dead man came out, his hands and feet wrapped with strips of linen, and a cloth around his face."[22] *Jesus calls the dead to life*. And when He does, dead men walk. After we intercede and move away hindrances by meeting the needs of others, we must trust Jesus to call the dead to life. It is Jesus and Jesus alone who can accomplish this feat.

When Lazarus responds to Jesus' voice and comes out of the tomb, Jesus then tells the people, "Take off the grave clothes and let him go."[23] Just as Jesus commands us to "make disciples," our third task in ministry is to do this by *taking off the death linens*, so that the new creation in Christ can be revealed. After Jesus raises Lazarus from the dead, He withdraws to Ephraim with his disciples. Then, "six days before the Passover, Jesus arrived at Bethany, where Lazarus lived, who Jesus had raised from the dead. Here a dinner was given in Jesus' honor. Martha served while Lazarus was among those reclining at the table with him."[24] This passage shows that Jesus had an ongoing relationship with Lazarus after he brought him from physical death to physical life. Likewise, in our ministries when the spiritually dead are brought to life, we, too, must have ongoing relationships with them to teach them how to grow in Christ.

> **The prevailing purpose of ministry is that God be glorified. The byproducts are that people come to know Christ and grow in Christ.**

The prevailing purpose of ministry is that God be glorified. The byproducts are that people come to know Christ and grow in Christ. God is the One who is glorified. He is the One who awakens the dead to life. He enables us to partner with Him: to intercede for the dead, to roll away the stones that block Jesus' voice, to minister to people based on their needs, to trust Jesus to call the dead to life, and, once Jesus has made them spiritually alive, take off death linens, thus revealing the new creation in Christ.

Principles of Evangelism Partnership with Christ
John 11: 1- 44

Purpose

- To Glorify the Father & Son
  vs. 4,14,40-41 - Jesus
- Interceding for Spiritually Dead
  vs. 17-36 - Us
- Rolling Away Stones
  v. 19 - Us
- Call the Dead to Life
  v. 43 - Jesus
- Taking off the Death Linens and let them go to do the same
  v. 44 - Us

> "It has become widely accepted that the far-reaching purpose of the gospel of Jesus Christ is to save me. It's all about my sin and how much God loved me and gave his only Son to die upon a cross-for me...But here's the question: is the gospel only about little, old me, or is it about something bigger? It's about something much bigger. Jesus made the clearest pronouncement that His work was for the glory of God: 'I glorified thee on earth, having accomplished the work which Thou hast given me to do' (John 17:4). Jesus also said that the fruit of the gospel in the Christian life has as its purpose the glory of God: 'by this is My Father glorified, that you bear much fruit, and so prove to be My disciples.' (John 15:8)... There is not a single verse in the Bible that says our joy in the Christian life is the gospel's ultimate concern. You can't find a verse saying our salvation is the end-all of God's plan. However, the Bible is replete with verse after verse pointing to God's own glory as the whole reason behind the work of Christ. In the end the gospel not for our glory—even for our salvation. It's for the glory of God...The Bible teaches that not only is the gospel designed to glorify God, but also everything that is in the world is here for the specific purpose of glorifying the Creator."[25]
>
> –John Barber, *Earth Restored*

McCown Sport in Ministry Map- Engel Scale

Discipleship-Presence of Christ in Sport

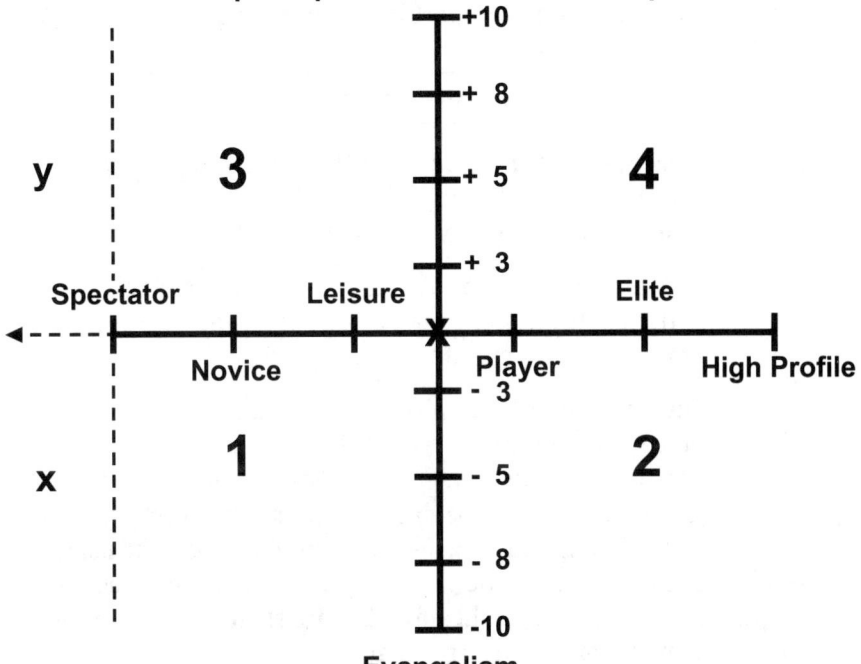

```
                    +10
                    + 8
      3             + 5            4
                    + 3
y
Spectator    Leisure         Elite
◄----+--------+--------X--------+--------+
           Novice      Player      High Profile
                    - 3
x     1             - 5            2
                    - 8
                    -10
```

Evangelism
Presenting Christ Through Sports

The blueprint of ministry outlined in this story happens along the spiritual continuum that forms the vertical axis on the Sport in Ministry Map. We are called to partner with God in ministry. Your ministry can intersect anywhere on this continuum. Depending on the spiritual needs of the people to whom you are ministering, you may be called to move stones while others are called to take off death linens. Whatever your situation, remember that no one point on this axis is better than another. Helping people progress upward from any point on the continuum is a vital ministry. Intercession for the spiritually dead and stone removal is necessary at the lower half of the continuum. The middle of the spiritual continuum, the "X" where the change of allegiance is made, is not more important than any other place. It is just the point where the spiritually dead are brought to spiritual life. There is still more to the journey. The death clothes still need to be taken off so the new creation can be revealed.

> We are called to partner with God in ministry.

CHAPTER FOUR

The following chapter explains how to use the Sport in Ministry Map. Chapter 8 will further develop the concept of partnership in ministry in which Christ invites us to take part.

Questions to think about:

1. Name someone that you know that is: A Spectator, Novice, Leisure, Player, Elite, High Profile. Do they have similar characteristics to the ones described in this chapter?

2. How are the needs of Spectators, Novices, and Leisure participants different than those of Players, Elite and High Profile? Why is important to know what they need?

3. The Engel Scale, the spiritual continuum, represents the process of growing toward Christ and growing in Christ. How would ministering to someone who has no idea that there is a God, -10, be different from ministering to some one who has heard the gospel before but has not made a commitment, -5? How would your ministry approach be different? How would you integrate their sport experience to minister to their spiritual needs?

4. What is the subtle difference between thinking that some one is a "non-believer" and thinking that someone is a "not yet believer?" How does thinking of people as "not yet believers" change your attitudes and actions toward people who are "not yet believers"?

5. It is amazing that God enables us to partner with Him in ministry to bring glory to Himself. What role have you played in ministry- Interceding? Rolling away stone? Taking off death linens? What did it entail?

6. Think of practical ways that you can:
   a. Intercede (pray for growth toward or growth in Jesus) for the people of sport.
   b. Roll away stones (so people can hear Jesus' voice) in the sport activity.
   c. Take off death linens (release them to be fully alive in Christ) in the sport experience.

In the Cross Hairs–
How to Use the McCown Sport in Ministry Map

CHAPTER FIVE

What is the purpose of sport in ministry? The purpose is to ultimately glorify God by helping the *people of sport* to grow toward and in Christlikeness. The first step is to consider how best to minister to them. Knowing where they are in their sport experience and where they are spiritually will help you determine the most effective approach to ministry. This chapter examines the basic approaches to sport in ministry and explains how to use the Sport in Ministry Map.

Approaches to Sport Ministry Target Audiences

The fundamental approach to sport in ministry is a *sport-valued approach*. Sport in ministry values sport and recognizes sport as the shared value of people of sport. The approach to people on the left side of the Map, Quadrants 1 and 3, involves the presentation of Christ through the use of sport stories, sport concepts, or testimonies. Through a sport story or example, a biblical concept is conveyed, and the Spectator, Novice, and Leisure participants have a common story to relate to. Through the story and the biblical concept there is an application made to spiritual life. Most sport devotionals, biographies and material to date are written for people on the left side of the Sport in Ministry Map.

> **What is the purpose of sport in ministry? The purpose is to ultimately glorify God by helping the people of sport to grow toward and in Christlikeness.**

An example of this approach, entitled, "Save" is from a sport devotional book by Curtis French:

Save

"For the Son of man is come to seek and to save that which was lost." –Luke 19:10

"A great defensive play in the closing moments of a contest is apt to provoke the comment, "that saved us." A game saving tackle or interception, a blocked shot, or a great catch with glove extended above the outfield wall are all part of the drama of sport...Often the performance of one great player is said to have saved a team from a disastrous season...To save a game or even a team from imminent defeat is one thing. But to save a soul and restore a life, that's really something else! Jesus Christ spoke the words that introduced this winning word...his primary state purpose was "to seek and to save that which was lost. Who are the lost whom Jesus says he came to save? To be lost is the opposite of being found. Has the love and unmerited favor (grace) of God found you? Or are you still lost, living an aimless life selfishly under your own direction? Christ came to save you, to put you into his record book, the Book of life. Respond to Christ's invitation! Whosoever shall call upon the name of the Lord shall be saved" (Rom. 10:13). Let Christ record another "save" by giving him your life."[1]

Notice this approach uses the sport concept as common ground that the reader can relate to. This is an attractive approach for Quadrants 1-3 because even though the Spectator, Novice, and Leisure person may not have ever experienced "a game saving" experience they relate vicariously to this story. The life application in this approach is a spiritual application. It does not personally connect to one's sport experience nor is there a practical application in sport. Since the left side of the Sport in Ministry Map incorporates the majority of people, there are great opportunities, programs, special events and literature to create mass appeal.

For Players, quadrants 2 and 4, on the right side of the Map, sport performance is critical. Their identity is defined as their performance in sport. Since everything is filtered through their sport worldview, it is important that they know and can experience how to apply spiritual principles where they live—in their sport experience. The effective approach for ministry to Players, Elite, and High Profile begins with the common ground of their own personal sport experience. In the context of their sport experience, a biblical truth is applied, thus leading to a life application through their experience of sport or a sport life application. Since their identity comes from their performance in sport, the most effective means to minister to them is to have them apply biblical principles directly to their sport experience.

The following is an example of a small group sport discussion written to the heart of the player in their sport experience.

Injury[2]

The Sport Experience
- What is the most difficult injury you have ever had to deal with in sport?
- How did the injury impact you?

The Bridge
- Tell a story of when you have seen someone over come an injury.
- What characteristics did you see in the person who overcame a serious injury?
- Have you ever seen good come from an injury?
- Read II Corinthians 12:7-10

The Connection
- Why would someone cry out to God when injured?
- How might this experience impact how you deal with injury in the future?

The Discovery
- What lessons have you learned from injury that could apply to your life?

CHAPTER FIVE

McCown Sport in Ministry Map - Engel Scale

Discipleship-Presence of Christ in Sport

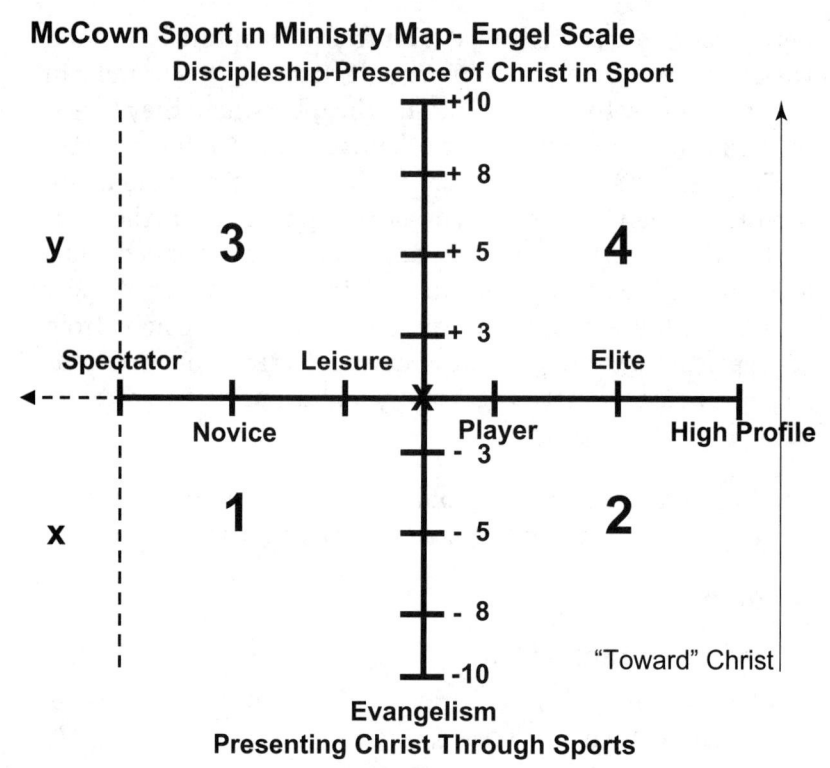

```
                    +10
                    + 8
    y       3       + 5       4
                    + 3
         Spectator  Leisure    Elite
    ◄ ---+---------+---------X---------+---------+──►
          Novice           Player            High Profile
                    - 3
    x       1       - 5       2
                    - 8
                   -10          "Toward" Christ
```

Evangelism
Presenting Christ Through Sports

Notice the difference between the two approaches. The approach for the people on the left side of the Map, Quadrants 1 and 3, utilizes a sport story or sport concept as common ground to capture the attention of the audience. The approach for the people on the right side of the Map, Quadrants 2 and 4, uses the reality of the sport experience to personally relate to one's own experience. Biblical truth has immediate relevance and impact which enables the person to see, try out, practice, and experience truth by experiencing the results for himself. As sport people are "going through life" they can apply biblical principles in the crucible of sport experience. This provides a direct connection between the biblical truth and what the sportsperson is experiencing.

Applying the philosophy of sport in ministry to this approach, it is through *experience* that *understanding* takes place. Once the people of sport *integrate* the biblical principles, in their sport experience they will *commit* to Christ.

Approaches to Sport in Ministry Target Audiences

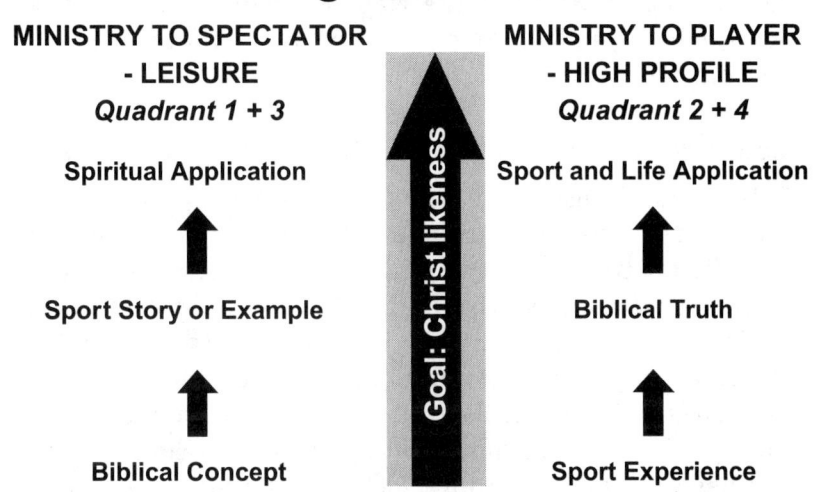

MINISTRY TO SPECTATOR - LEISURE
Quadrant 1 + 3

Spiritual Application
↑
Sport Story or Example
↑
Biblical Concept

Goal: Christ likeness

MINISTRY TO PLAYER - HIGH PROFILE
Quadrant 2 + 4

Sport and Life Application
↑
Biblical Truth
↑
Sport Experience

While the sport story approach is appropriate for Quadrants 1 and 3 ministries, it is not effective for Quadrants 2 and 4 because it does not directly apply to growth in Christ *within* their experience of sport.

The sport experience is an ideal place for not yet believers to test the truth of the gospel. Not only is the sport experience valuable for not yet believers, it is also valuable because it allows believers to live out the truth within their sport. In this way they can grow in Christ as they practice the Presence of Christ through demonstration, proclamation, experience, and integration in the activity of sport. The gospel lived out in and through sport will ultimately lead to transformed lives. Currently there is very little written to address the specific needs of people in quadrants 2 and 4.

In the Cross Hairs

A cross hair is a thin wire located in the eyepiece of an optical instrument. Usually there are two intersecting wires as seen through a telescope that serve as a focus point. Cross hairs are also used on an airplane instrument panel serving as horizontal and vertical reference points for the

> **The gospel lived out in and through sport will ultimately lead to transformed lives.**

pilot. The Sport in Ministry Map helps you locate your target audience through the use of cross hairs. The location of your target audience on the Map will serve as a reference point to help you focus in on the most appropriate approach for your ministry.

Learning How to Use the Map

To learn how to use the map, locate where you would fall on the sport experience continuum. The sport valued approach to ministry always starts with the sport experience. Put your pen on that spot on the horizontal continuum. Using a straight edge, draw a vertical line that bisects the spot on the sport experience continuum. Next, locate where you would be on the spiritual continuum. Draw a horizontal line through that spot on the vertical continuum. The two lines you have drawn should intersect and look like cross hairs on a telescope. The place where the lines intersect is your location on the Sport in Ministry Map. Mark the intersection drawing a small circle around where the lines intersect.

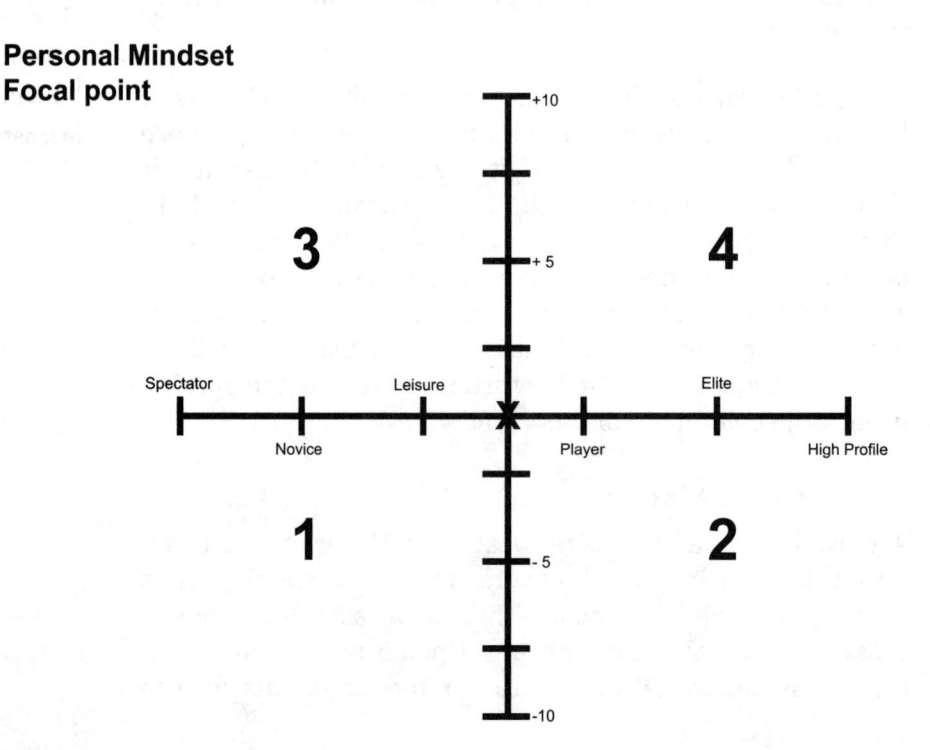

Personal Mindset
Focal point

Practice Using the Map

To practice using the map, follow the diagrammed example of ministry for four players. Player A has all the characteristics of a Player and quite a few characteristics of an Elite player. She is located just to the left of the Elite mark on the Map. A vertical line is drawn through that spot. Spiritually, Player A has previously heard about the birth, death, and resurrection of Christ, but as yet it has no personal significance or meaning to her. She is diagnosed as a -5 on the spiritual continuum and a horizontal line is drawn through the -5 spot on the Map. The cross hairs, where the two lines intersect, is Player A's location on the Map.

Player B has all the characteristics of a Player and has a few Elite characteristics. She is located one-third of the distance between the Player and Elite categories on the sport experience continuum. A vertical line is drawn through this spot on the horizontal continuum. Spiritually, Player B recognizes the problem of sin in her life and the need for repentance but has not had a change of allegiance yet. The horizontal line is drawn through the -2 on the Map. Locate Player B's spot on the map through the cross hairs.

Since Player C is a Player without any of the characteristics of an Elite, a vertical line is drawn directly

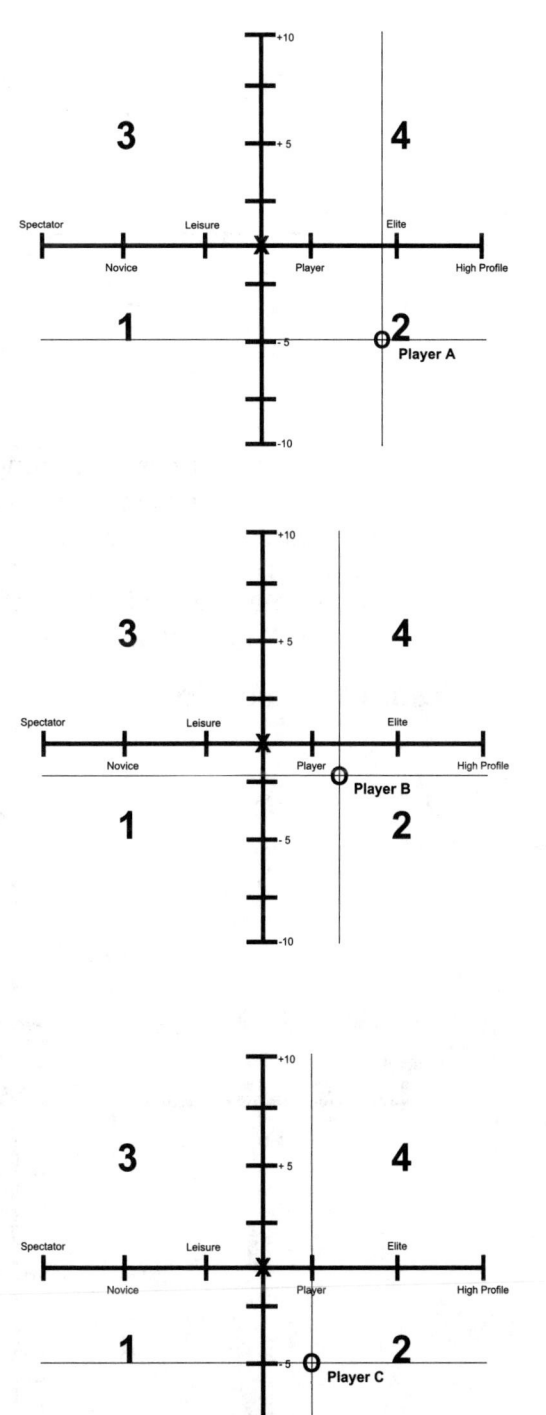

CHAPTER FIVE

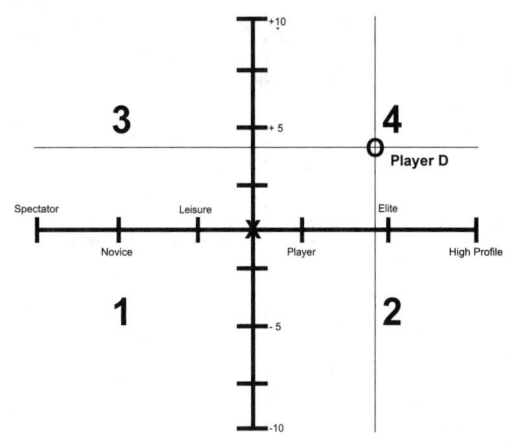

through the Player mark. She understands that Jesus was a good man but does not know the truth of the gospel yet. A line is drawn horizontally through the -5. See where Player C is plotted on the Map.

Player D has most of the characteristics of an Elite player and has had a change of allegiance. She is growing in her relationship with Christ, actively serves in her local church and has a yearning to know how her faith relates to her sport experience. Take note of where the cross hairs locate Player D on the Map.

Once all individuals in the target audience are plotted on the Map, a shape encircling all four players on the Map is

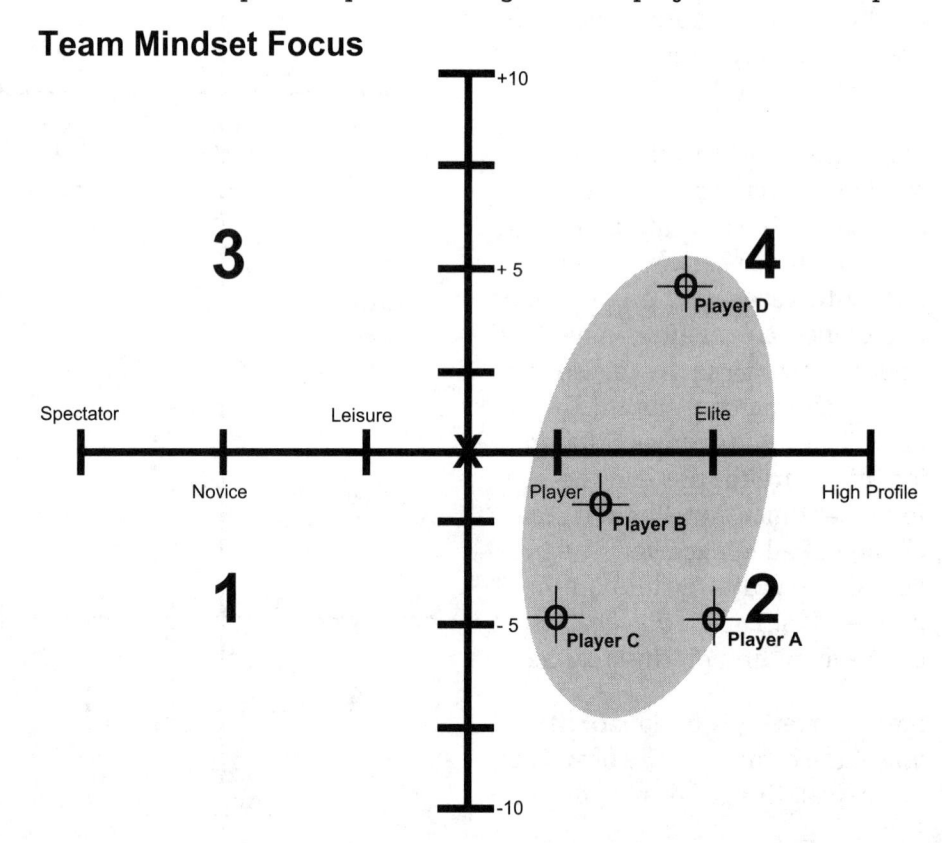

Team Mindset Focus

drawn. The shape that surrounds all four people outlines where this target audience is located on the Map.

How the Map Works – Focus on Your Target Audience

Who are you trying to reach in your sport in ministry? To whom is God calling you to minister? What are the needs of the sportspeople you want to reach? If you want to minister to High Profile players, but do not have access to them nor are there any major professional teams in your city, perhaps that group is not where God is calling you to reach. It is important that you seek God's call and clearly identify which group of people your ministry will focus on.

Once you have identified the group of people to minister to, you must determine where they are in their sport experience. Which category best describes their experience in sport? First, identify on the map where they would be on the

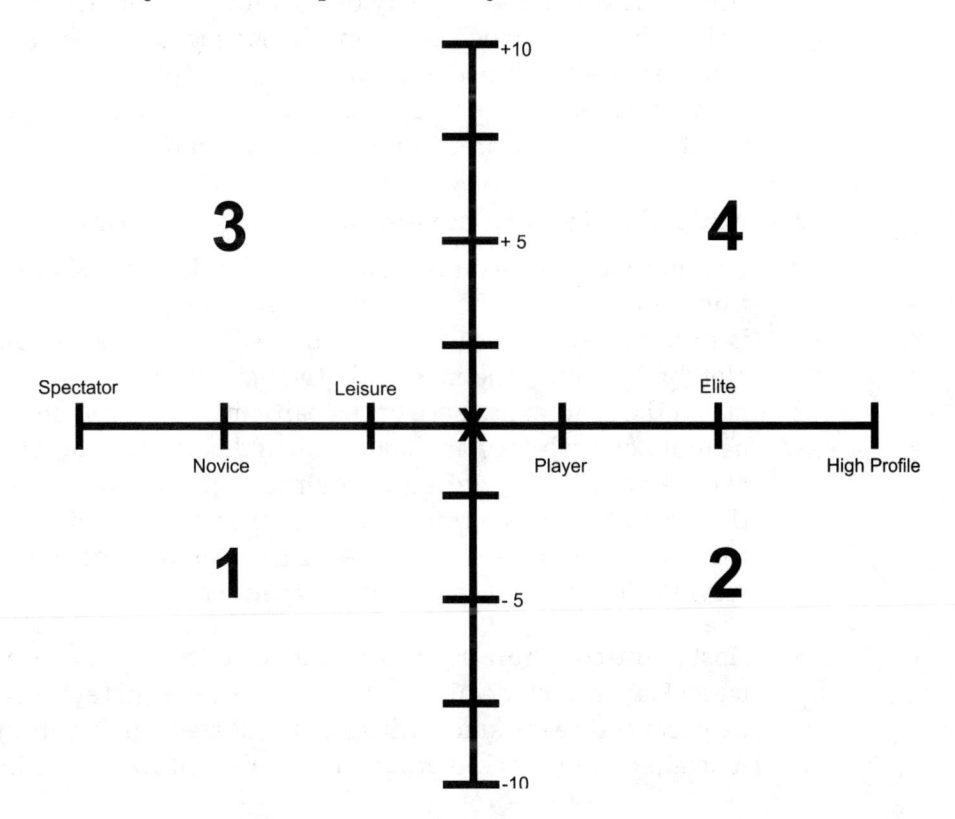

```
                         +10
                          |
                          |
          3               |+5           4
                          |
                          |
 Spectator      Leisure   |        Elite
 |------|----------|------*------|---------|
         Novice           |   Player    High Profile
                          |
          1               |-5           2
                          |
                          |
                          |-10
```

horizontal continuum. Next, think about where the people you want to serve are spiritually. Have they come to know Christ yet? Consider where they are spiritually and identify on the map where these people are on the vertical continuum. Following the same procedures used in the example of the four players, identify where each individual would be in your target audience. Locate using cross hairs where each person would be in your group on the Map. After each person is illustrated draw a shape that includes all the spots on the Map. This is the location of your target audience on the Map. The shaped outline on the Map shows the breadth of your target audience but does not show volume or size of the ministry.

If your target audience is large, think of the range of people in the group. Would the majority of the people be Novices or Players? Are they believers or not yet believers? You can represent a large group of people by drawing a shape that surrounds where the majority of the group would be. If your group spans too much area on the Map you will want to consider how to narrow your focus of ministry. Bigger is not necessarily better since effective ministry requires appropriate approaches for different target audiences.

Matching Map Location and Ministry Model

Working with people on the left side of the Map differs greatly from working with the right side of the Map. The approach is different and the ministry model will therefore be completely different. The most effective ministries will seek to match the sport experience of the participants. Players should be grouped with Players. Novices should be placed together. Leisure should play with and against other Leisure people. Unfortunately, what often happens in a church setting is that as we try to meet the needs of the majority and end up serving the lowest level of sport experience.

Most ministries run a Leisure league, although there are many Players included in the target audience. This approach neglects the needs and abilities of the Players in the group. A smaller more specific program geared for different ability

> **Bigger is not necessarily better since effective ministry requires appropriate approaches for different target audiences.**

levels is more beneficial and attractive than one program that tries to fit everyone. One size does not fit all.

Where Challenge Meets Ability

There is a concept in sport psychology called "flow." Flow is achieved when the challenge of the sport matches the ability of the participant. For a Player, that is the pinnacle of a positive sport experience. There is a flow of exhilaration when one's sporting ability reaches the demands of competition. However, if the challenge is too great for one's ability level, anxiety is produced. That is, if someone is playing in a league or competition that is too challenging, anxiety is the outcome. So the Leisure player that plays in a league that is too difficult for his abilities (see diagram, Person A) becomes fraught with anxiety. On the other hand, if the challenge is too low for one's ability level, boredom results. An Elite player who plays in a Leisure league does not get his need to improve his performance met because the level of play is not sufficiently challenging (Person B). In an effort to meet the needs of the people in your program, it is imperative that sport in ministry specialize in matching ability levels of the participants with the challenge of the competition (Person C).

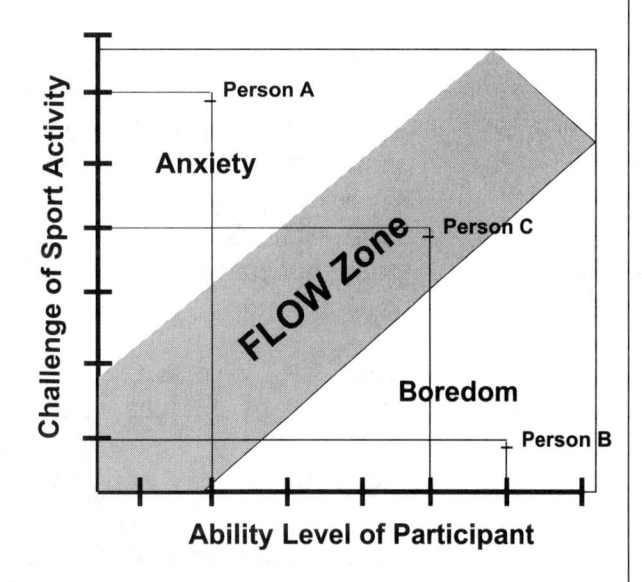

> There is a flow of exhilaration when one's sport ability reaches the demands of competition.

Mapping out Models of Ministry

Currently there are well over 100 different models sport ministry in the world. Each model and their target audience can be charted on the Map. Each model can be charted by finding the location of the target audiences on the sport experience and spiritual continuums. In an effort to illustrate the breadth and depth of sport in ministry, the following case statements are offered for practice in using the Sport

CHAPTER FIVE

in Ministry Map. These case statements represent actual ministries that were birthed out of the hearts of people in specific cultural contexts. These ministries considered the needs, interests, and situations and implemented it to meet the needs of people of sport. It is our hope that these models will excite ideas in your heart and mind, not for duplication, but to cast a vision unique to your situation, ministry, and culture.

Read each case statement carefully. Using the instructions outlined in this chapter, plot out the target audience for each ministry. The case statements are plotted out on the Sport in Ministry Map at the end of the book.

Case Statement # 1 - Europe

A church in the heart of one of the least evangelized cities in Europe remodeled their courtyard into a basketball court. Their plan was to host clinics and leagues to reach out to the 20,000 homes in the surrounding community. Their

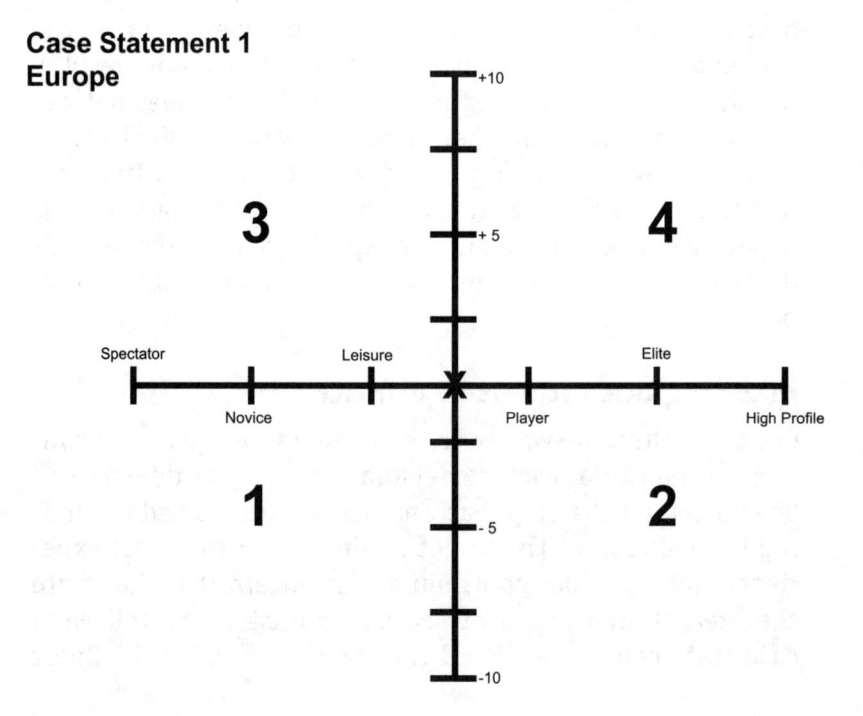

Case Statement 1
Europe

country has only been given freedom to worship in recent years consequently there are few evangelical churches, with most averaging under 100 members each.

Basketball is the second most popular sport in the city behind football (soccer). The church has been very aggressive in reaching out to the community through door to door campaigns, music and dramas in the parks. Yet after all their efforts only a couple of new families joined their church over the last 10 years.

During a major sports event in their city they hosted several basketball clinics for their community. They partnered with a sports ministry who provided the coaching expertise. They hosted two clinics involving several hundred youth from the neighborhood who had no connection with the church before. As a direct result of clinics five new families joined the church making this the most effective community outreach they had ever held.

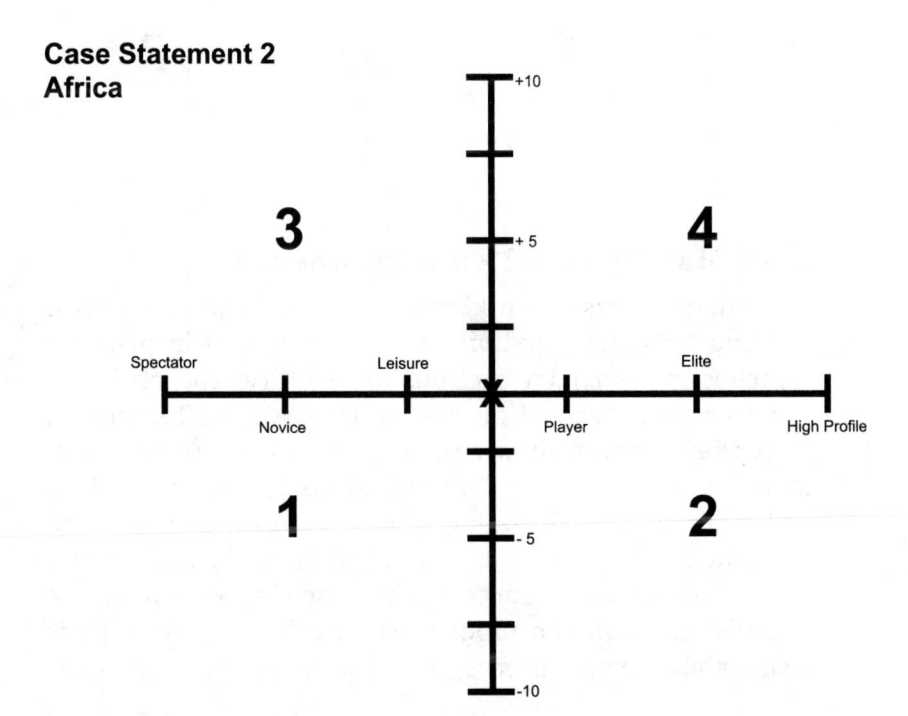

Case Statement 2
Africa

Case Statement # 2 - Africa

A church in the inner city the capital of a central African country became aware of the serious problem of homeless street children. To build relationships with the children the churched began a special basketball league for them. The league was so successful that they found they could do more to assist the children and youth. Over 600 children were placed into foster homes.

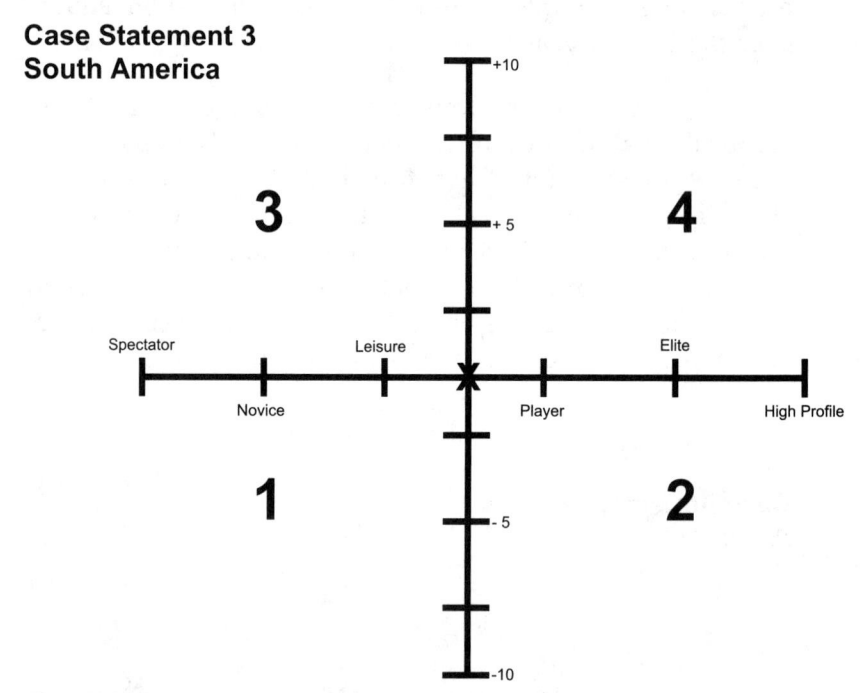

**Case Statement 3
South America**

```
                        +10
               3                  4
                        +5

  Spectator      Leisure              Elite
  ├──────┼──────┼──────✕──────┼──────┼──────┤
           Novice         Player        High Profile

               1          -5      2

                        -10
```

Case Statement # 3 - South America

A Seminary professor working in a very difficult city known for drug trafficking and violence was involved in planting churches in very poor sections of the city. The professor started a soccer school for the youth. Several afternoons a week they would train soccer players and teams. Each day they focused on soccer skill and strategy development as well as physical conditioning. They also incorporated a time spiritual training through time of bible study and prayer. Many of players experienced a change of allegiance and came to Christ through the program. Through the players their families also experienced spiritual growth. Three churches were soon planted in the communities where the players lived. The program now has a number of full time coaches, many of who came to know Christ as players in the program.

Case Statement # 4 - Sub Indian Continent

Many sportspeople are known to have a love for Christ, but find it difficult to mature in their faith while active in sport. In some parts of the country there is religious persecution. In several large cities Sport Chapters are begun to serve the sportspeople. They gather together regularly for Bible study, prayer and fellowship to discuss the issues they face in sport and life.

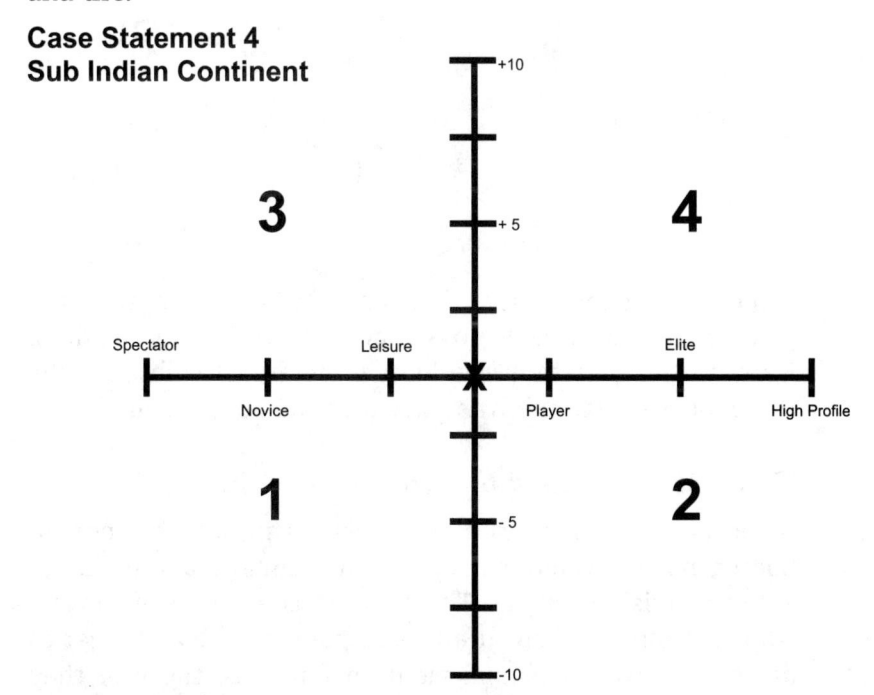

**Case Statement 4
Sub Indian Continent**

```
                        +10
            3                      4
                        +5

   Spectator      Leisure              Elite
   ├──────────────┼──────X──────┼──────────────┤
           Novice        Player        High Profile

            1                      2
                        -5


                        -10
```

Case Statement # 5 - Latin America

In a soccer dominated culture of a central American country a Pastor who is a retired elite professional player, plants a church based on small group ministry through soccer teams. He organizes leagues where the teams are comprised of house groups (small groups). In order to play you have to attend weekly small group bible studies where game jerseys are distributed for the games that week.

**Case Statement 5
Latin America**

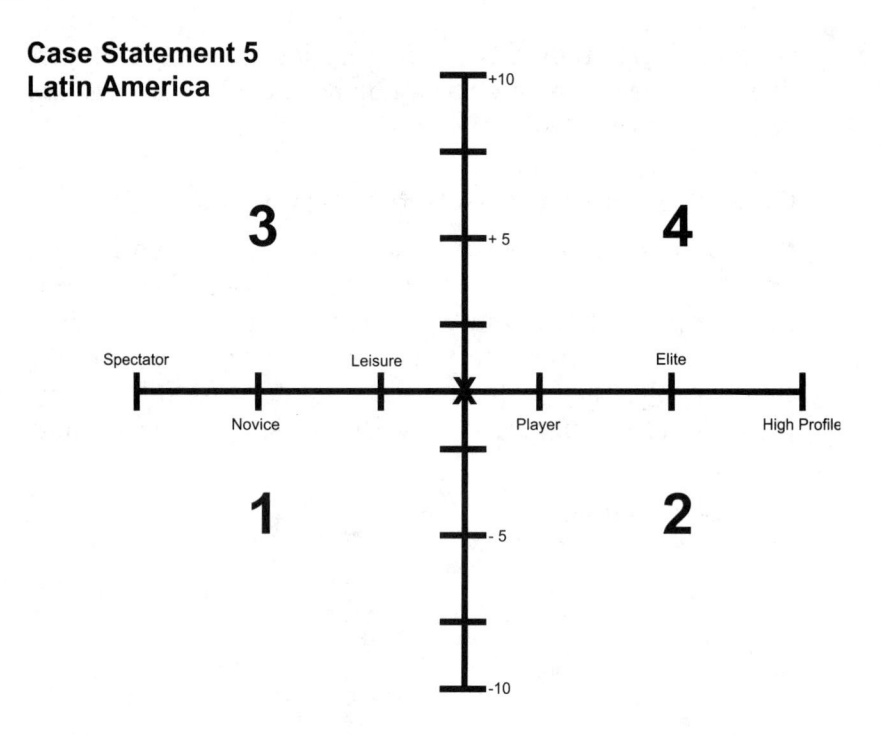

```
                    +10
                     |
                     |
         3           |           4
                    +5
                     |
                     |
Spectator      Leisure |         Elite
————+——————+——————X——————+——————+————
         Novice      |  Player          High Profile
                     |
                     |
         1          -5           2
                     |
                     |
                   -10
```

A special worship service is held on Tuesday evenings, for the players who are unable to attend regular Sunday services. Many top players from the local professional clubs and the National team attend. It is known as the Soccer Church.

Case Statement # 6 - North America

A sports ministry focused on ministry through the sport of Soccer, purchase and manage a professional team to play in a third division league. The team is comprised of players who love Christ. Their intent is to play in such a manner to demonstrate their commitment to Christ in the way they play, relate to each other and interact with opponents, referees and spectators.

The following chapter rolls out the modern history of sport in ministry giving a brief overview of where sport ministry has been and the unlimited opportunities for sport in ministry in the future.

Case Statement 6
North America

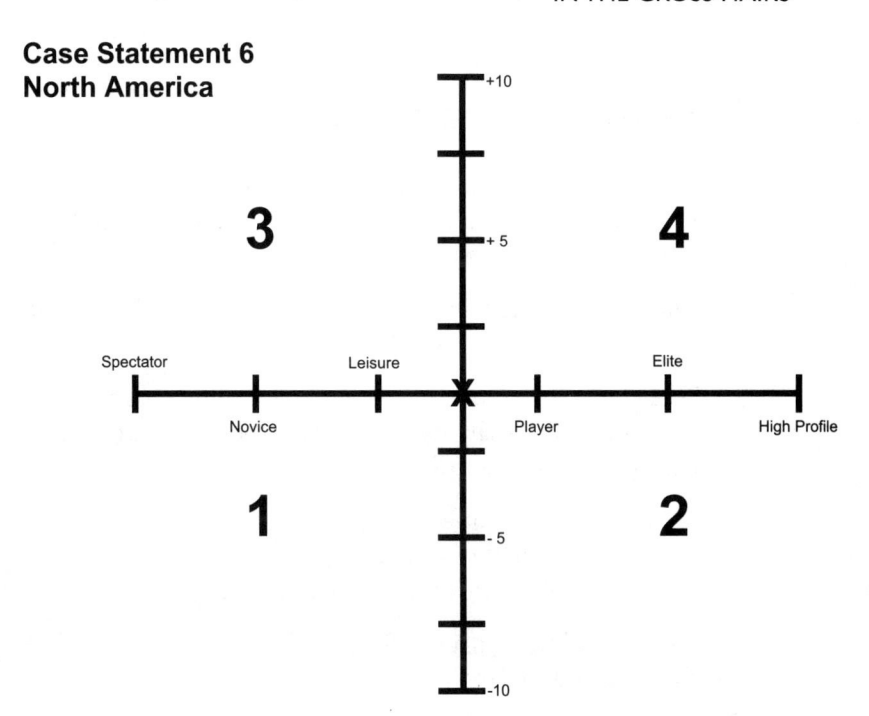

```
              +10
               |
        3      |      4
               + 5
               |
Spectator   Leisure    Elite
 |----+------+------✗------+------+----|
       Novice       Player      High Profile
               |
        1      |      2
               - 5
               |
              -10
```

Questions to think about:

1. How does the heart of a Player differ from the heart of a Leisure participant? Which approach would you use to minister to these two people?

2. How does a sport-valued approach to ministry differ from sports evangelism?

3. Where are the people on the Map you want to minister to or be involved with? What are the needs and interests of that particular group?

4. Can you think of an experience in sport that a biblical truth can be applied to that could be experienced and integrated by a person in the activity of sport?

5. What would the sports world be like if believers integrated the Presence of Christ in the sport experience?

6. How can you ensure that the challenge of the sport activity meets the ability levels of the people you are working with? What adjustments will you need to make in order to effectively minister to everyone in your group?

7. What cultural situations are unique to your situation that you will need to be mindful of?

8. What vision for Sport in Ministry is God birthing in your heart?

Past Perspectives and Trends in Sports Ministry

CHAPTER SIX

It is crucial to understand the past perspectives and trends of sports ministry to understand where we are today and how to strategically think about the future. Where did sports ministry begin? What motivated and influenced the pioneers of the modern movement of sports ministry? What can we learn from the past? We will look give a cursory look at sport and the early Church and give a brief outline of the history of sports ministry. Though the authors recognize that many ministries have had a role in history, it is not our intent to list every ministry here. Instead, the past is summarized through the presentation of representative trends, highlighting the pioneer ministries of each. Each of the trends mentioned have also been diagrammed on the Sport in Ministry Map to show the general direction in which it developed.

Sport and the Early Church

We do not know for sure how the early Church felt about sport, but we do know that the apostle Paul saw sports as an effective way to illustrate biblical principles. As the synagogue in Corinth where he preached is located close to the site where the Isthmus Games were held, it is reasonable to

> We do not know for sure how the early Church felt about sport, but we do know that the apostle Paul saw sports as an effective way to illustrate biblical principles.

assume that his audience was familiar with sport and likely held no negative views of sport. For had this been the case, Paul probably would not have chosen powerful sport metaphors to connect with his readers, "Do you know that in a race all the runners run, but only one gets the prize? Run in such a way as to get the prize. Everyone who competes in the games goes into strict training. They do it to get a crown that will not last, but we do it to get a crown that will last forever."[1] The details in phrases such as "running the race" and a "crown that will not last," (a reference describing a wreath of wild celery given to the victors of the Games) seem to suggest a first-hand account of the events which Paul may have even witnessed himself.

> **The Church separated the sacred from the secular, forgetting the Hebrew worldview that embraced all of life holistically the body and mind as one.**

Though at the time of Paul's writing to the Corinthians there were no negative connotations associated with sport, sport did present a problematic issue for the Church as the Roman spectacles became increasingly violent. As a result, the Church condemned sport. During the second century, Tertullian of Carthage put a halt to sport competitions due to the fatalities from violence in the gladiator games and other bloody exhibitions.[2] Greek theologian Clementine of Alexandra, the first Christian Roman emperor, promoted Greek dualism, which thought, since the body was evil, sport was evil, too. Greek dualism separates the mind and the body, coveting the mind (sacred) and devaluing the body (secular). Likewise, the Church separated the sacred from the secular, forgetting the Hebrew worldview that embraced all of life holistically—the body and mind as one. This dualistic philosophy greatly influenced the history of the church and still haunts us today. Many believe that God is exclusively concerned about religious activities, forgetting that God is the God of all creation, sacred and secular. All of life is under His dominion and concern. Theologian John Stott said, "Our God is often too small because he is too religious. We imagine that He is chiefly interested in religion—in religious buildings, religious activities and religious books. Of course He is concerned about these things, but only if they are related to the whole of life. According to the Old Testament prophets and the teaching of Jesus, God is very critical of 'religion,' if by that is meant religious services divorced from real life, loving service, and the moral obedience of the heart."[3]

Unfortunately, believers throughout history did not have an influence in the world of sport. While the culture around them was impacting and shaping sport, as reviewed in chapter one, the Church had no influence on sport because believers had pulled out of the sports world. It was not until the early 1800's that believers began to see sport as a way to build character in young people. This was the birth of sports ministry.

Character Building

In 1828, Dr. Tom Arnold began The School of Rugby, the first sports ministry in England, established to build Christian character in young boys. This character building trend continued in 1844, with Sir George Williams' founding of the Young Men's Christian Association (YMCA), ministry aimed at developing the total man through Bible study, prayers and physical activities. Physical exercise and activities were considered effective means for developing Christian character. The fourfold purpose of the YMCA adopted in 1866, "The improvement of the spiritual, mental, social and physical condition of young men."[4] This was seen in the birth of the sport of basketball during the winter of 1891 as an "athletic distraction" to remedy behavior in class of rowdy boys.[5] During this same period, another trend of sports ministry began, which focused on "top" sportspeople, or "muscular Christians," using their athletic fame to promote the gospel.

Muscular Christianity

The phrase "Muscular Christianity" expresses the idea of physical strength and vigor as a characteristic of those who are strong in the Lord. The term was coined in Great Britain when three of England's most famous Cricket players—brothers Charles (a.k.a. "CT"), Kynaston, and George Studd—had a change of allegiance to Jesus, launching the muscular Christianity movement in sports ministry. Never before had

> The phrase "Muscular Christianity" expresses the idea of physical strength and vigor as characteristic of those who are strong in the Lord.

such famous sportsmen used their sports notoriety to share Christ. "C.T.", recognized as the greatest Cricket player of all time, brought many to Christ including most of his teammates. In 1885, "CT" gave up his illustrious cricket career to become a missionary to China as a member of the famous Cambridge Seven, a missionary team that included all three Studd brothers and four others.

The Muscular Christianity movement quickly spread to the United States. In 1886, professional baseball player Billy Sunday had a change of allegiance to Christ. His significantly changed behavior drew much public attention. From 1886-1892 his stand for Christ, coupled with his illustrious baseball career, strengthened the growth of Muscular Christianity in the United States. Suddenly, in 1893, Sunday, previously advocate and teammate of muscular Christianity, became its outspoken opponent. Sunday prematurely ended his baseball career concluding that Christianity and sport were "mutually exclusive endeavors." He advocated that there was no value for sport except as a means to share the gospel.[6] His reasons for leaving baseball focused on negative aspects he saw in sport such as the selfishness and jealousy that sport breeds, time commitment that prevented him from study, and an "undeniable future" that sports leads to. Billy Sunday's beliefs that Christian values and professional sport were incompatible reverted back to a school of thought that echoed Greek dualism.

Team-Sending Model

The early 1950's introduced the new trend to sports ministry of team sending. At the same time, the movement of Christian Outreach, holding large evangelistic meetings, became a popular means to share the gospel. The idea of team sending was birthed when Dick Hollis and other missionaries in Taiwan witnessed hundreds of people walk right pass their street evangelism outreach into a basketball arena. Wanting to reach the multitudes for Christ, the missionaries came up with the idea of hosting a basketball game where testimonies of Christian players could be shared during the game. Madame Chiang Kai-shek, the wife of the president of

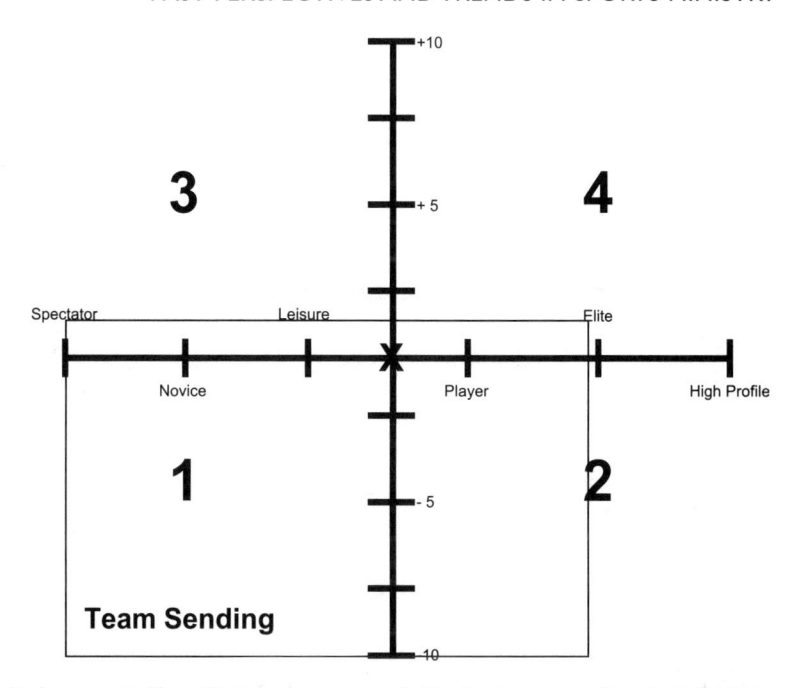

```
                    +10
                     |
                     |
        3            | +5           4
                     |
                     |
 Spectator    Leisure|         Elite
 |------|-----|------X------|----|------|
       Novice       Player        High Profile
                     |
        1            | -5           2
                     |
                     |
 Team Sending        |
                    -10
```

Taiwan at the time, supported their idea and extended an invitation to Taylor University basketball team. Taylor Coach Don Odle and his team played the Taiwan National team and over eighty-three other opponents in Taiwan during the summer of 1952. During half time at the games, the Taylor team gave a twenty-minute program featuring songs, testimonies, and an invitation to receive the gospel message.[7]

Following the model set by the Taylor basketball team, the first team-sending ministry was formed, called Ventures for Victory. Their target audience ranged from Spectator to Player, -10 to +1 on the Sport in Ministry Map (see Chapter 4). Another team-sending organization, Athletes in Action (AIA), was founded in 1966 for the purpose of sharing the gospel in front of their audience/fans at half time and then meeting with their opponents to talk and share after games. Their target audience was university-aged people of sport, Players to Elite, -5 to +2 and Spectators.

National Sport Ministry Model

In the United States, the second model of sports ministry in the 20th century, after team sending, was ministry groups to

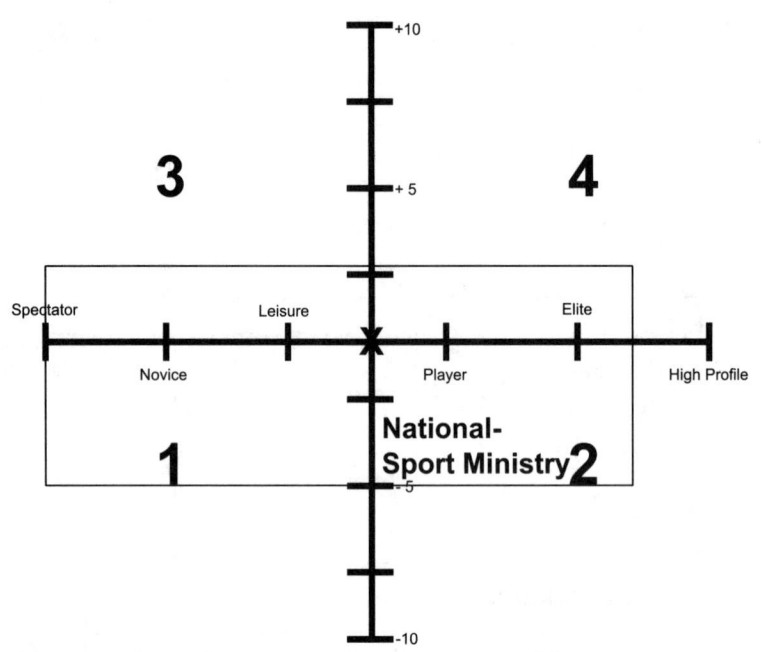

```
            +10
             |
    3        +5        4
             |
  ┌──────────┼──────────┐
  │Spectator Leisure  Elite│
──┼────┼─────✱─────┼────┼──
  │  Novice      Player  High Profile
  │       National-
  │  1    Sport Ministry  2
  └──────────┼──────────┘
            -5
             |
             |
            -10
```

athletes and coaches across the country. Weeklong sport camps were held for boys at the secondary and university levels. Sport rallies featuring testimonies of sport personalities were used to proclaim the gospel. Large group meetings included demonstrations of sport skills by athletes such as Paul Anderson ("the world's strongest man") demonstrating his feats of strength and sharing his testimony. The Fellowship of Christian Athletes (FCA), one of the more widely-recognized sports ministry models in the United States, was established in 1950 with a ministry focus on both Spectators and Players, ranging from -5 to +3 on the Map.

Church Sport and Recreation Model

There was a movement in church recreation as early as the 1920's that focused on creating opportunities for recreational fellowship for people in the church as well as evangelistic outreach to the community. This was a popular trend until the 1950's when recreational interests waned. In the 1970's there was a resurgence of recreational offerings in the church not only for recreational and social fellowship but for evangelistic outreach as well. The church sport and recreation trend has continued as indigenous churches see the impact and significance sport and recreation has on their communities. Sports ministries that are not mission agency-based are usually based in the local church. In 1995, an organization called the Church Sport Recreation Ministers (CSRM) began to develop an organization to network and support those who use recreation and sports as a ministry in the church.[8] This model targets primarily Leisure -6 to +3.

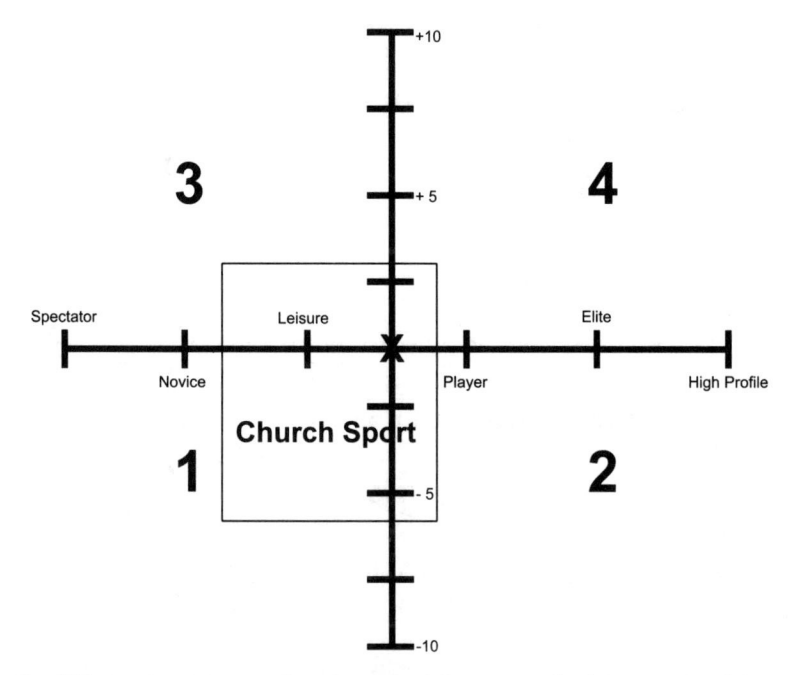

Major Sports Events Outreach Model

The Major Sports Events Outreach model capitalizes on the popularity of major sports events to distribute gospel literature to the people in attendance. The Major Sports Events Outreach targets Spectator to High Profile, -4 to +2. Gospel tracts, Christian literature, and Bibles are distributed at the events to promote the gospel. The trend for Major Sports Events Outreach started with the 1968 winter Olympics in Grenoble, France. Since then there have been major outreach events annually at most major international sport venues, including the Olympics, the FIFA World Cup, Super Bowl, and Rugby World Cup.

CHAPTER SIX

```
                    +10
                     |
                     |
          3          +5        4
                     |
Spectator      Leisure        Elite
——+——————+——————+—————★—————+——————+—— High Profile
            Novice        Player
         Major Sports Event Outreach
          1          -5        2
                     |
                     |
                    -10
```

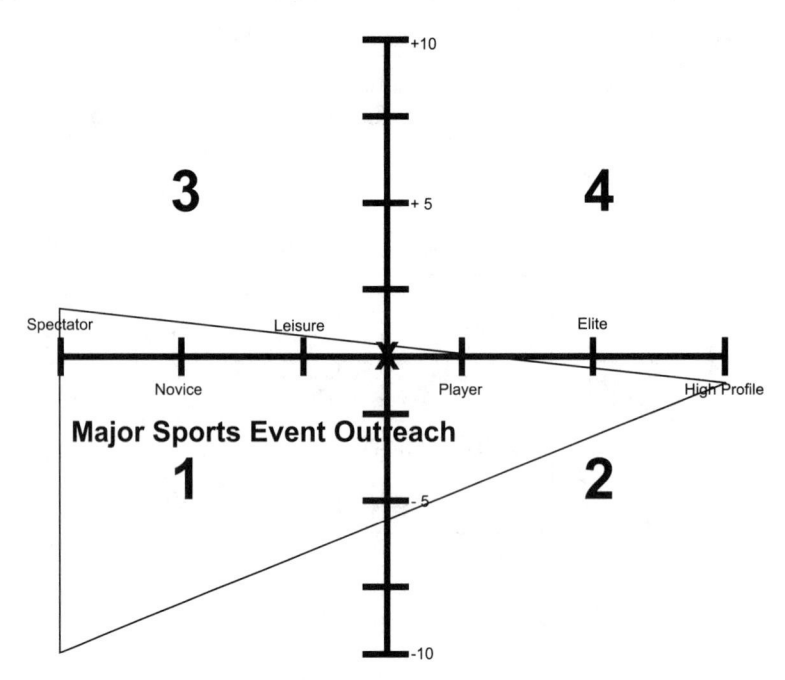

A new type of sport outreach model began at the 1988 Calgary Winter Olympics when the believers from Calgary decided not just to target the people attending the Olympics but focused on reaching out and ministering to their own neighboring communities through the Games. It was the first time that a sport outreach targeted the residents of the host city.

High-quality tracts and booklets, highlighting sport testimonies and an evangelistic message, were produced in 27 different languages for distribution to visitors and Olympic participants for the first time at the 1988 Seoul Olympics. During the 1990 FIFA World Cup in Italy, sports testimonies were featured in media broadcasts and in printed materials and handed out to visitors and participants. Churches and ministry agencies printed gospel tracts in partnership for World Cup distribution. Starting with the 1992 Super Bowl (American football), a kit containing a video of sports testimonies of professional football players and a special Super Bowl magazine, was produced and distributed to church groups. Believers invited their not yet believing friends to Super Bowl parties hosted at churches where together they would watch both the game and the outreach video. At the 1996 Olympics in Atlanta, 15 different evangelistic items such as booklets, videos, Bibles and other forms of literature were produced for 40 countries developed for distribution during the Games. At the 1998 FIFA World Cup in France, evangelistic materials for 114 countries were produced. The items designed for the 2000 Sydney Olympics included 24 different evangelistic materials produced for 90 countries. The items produced were geared towards people of sport, from Spectators to High Profile Players, -10 to +2.

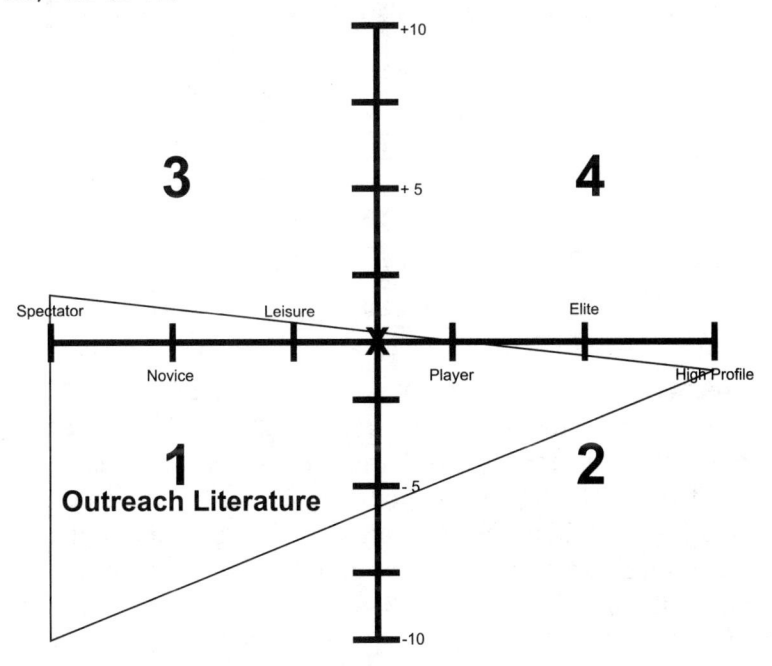

Specialized Sport Model

Sportler Ruft Sportler (now called SRS Pro Sportler), the first specialized sports ministry, began in Europe in 1969. They focus on helping people in twenty-six different sports, ranging in level from Player through High Profile players, to become better sportsmen and women in their specific sport. SRS members provide sport expertise while demonstrating the love of Christ through training, publications, and one-on-one relationships to High Profile players, and sport agents. The SRS target audience is mid Leisure to High Profile, -6 to +5.

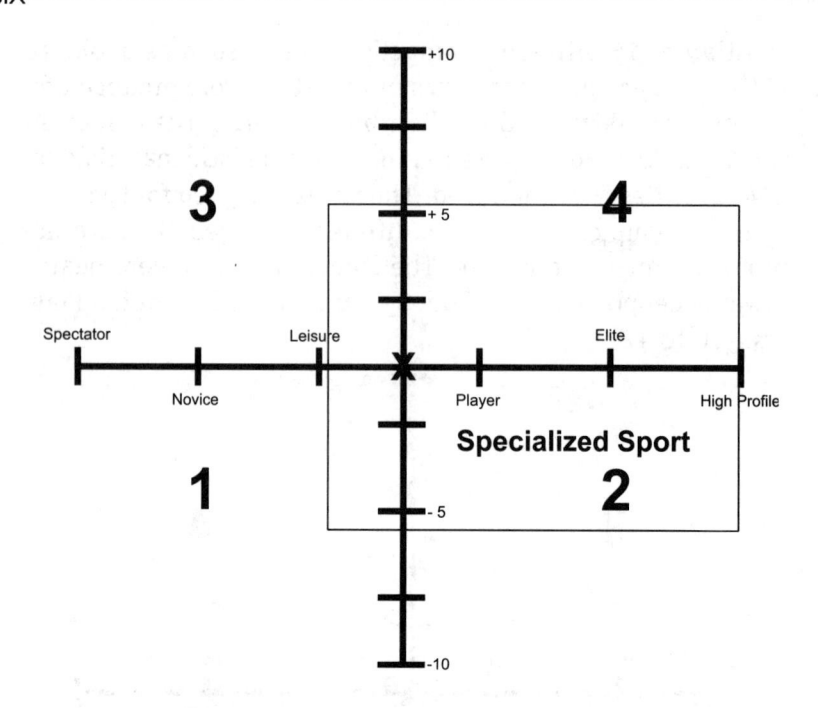

```
                        +10

            3                    4
                       +5

    Spectator    Leisure        Elite
    ├────────────┼──────X────────┼────────┤
         Novice        Player      High Profile
                            Specialized Sport
            1                    2
                       -5


                       -10
```

A second specialized sport model, Christians in Sport (CIS), began in England in 1972 through the leadership of top sportsmen. CIS mission is "reaching the world of sport for Christ–encouraging and supporting Christians to share the good news of Jesus with their sporting friends."[9] It is an indigenous sport ministry targeting high Leisure to Elite university people of sport, -4 to +4.

Outreach to High Profile Athletes

In 1971, Norm Evans felt he must be the only believer playing in the National (American) Football League. For though there were definitely other Christian professional (High Profile) football players in the League, they simply didn't know of each other; they had no network to connect them, no place to interact and share their faith. So after his retirement from professional (High Profile) sports, Evans began an outreach serving NFL players, a ministry which grew as a direct response to one player's heart–felt needs. Today, players meet for encouragement and to practice spiritual discipline. Similarly, players and their wives meet for Bible study and fellowship. This ministry, Pro Athletes Outreach (PAO), not only targets Elite to High Profile players, -2 to +5, but also their spouses.

In 1986 a group of committed believers had a vision to reach for Christ the futbol players on the 1994 Brazilian national team. The group, Atletas de Cristo, led by former Formula One driver Alex Ribeiro, began to pray for the prospective players on that team, and devised a strategy to reach top

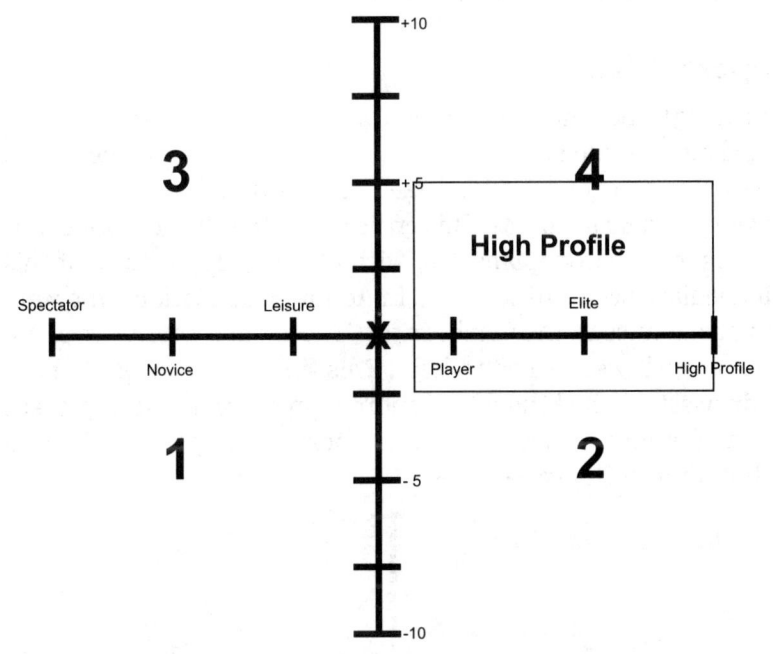

```
                    +10

         3                    4

                    +5
                          High Profile
  Spectator    Leisure        Elite
  |——————|——————|——————*——————|——————|——————|
              Novice        Player      High Profile

         1                    2
                    -5


                    -10
```

players for Christ. Their strategy included holding Monday night Bible studies led by a pastor in the homes of the potential players. Their prayers were first answered when five of the players recruited for the 1994 Brazilian FIFA World Cup team were believers. But little did they know that the God would use these five futbol players to make a powerful stand for Him as Brazil went on to win the World Cup. God chose not just to honor prayers for the salvation of Brazilian World Cup players alone, but to impact all who watched and took part in the World Cup.

But the story doesn't end with the team's capturing the coveted 1994 FIFA World Cup. In 1998 half of the evangelistic materials produced for the World Cup were developed from the Mediterranean region. Since there were not any High Profile believers from that part of the world, they partnered with the Atletas de Cristo group to produce eight different media and literature pieces showcasing the Brazilian futbol players. The literature and videos retold the story of the Brazilian believers who won the World Cup presenting the love of Christ to millions of people. The media and literature pieces were targeted for Spectators at a -5 to +2.

Sport Chaplaincy

Although the aim of the Olympics is to promote peace between nations through sport, in 1972 in Munich, Germany, the Games became a war zone. Eleven Israeli power lifters and weightlifters were killed by terrorists. This crisis prompted the need for counselors to help Olympians deal with the tragedy. Because of this immediate need, the Athletes In Action organization, who were in attendance at the Games in an "unofficial capacity" to share the gospel, were asked to help. This first model of sport chaplaincy established the role of sport chaplaincy has been present at all Olympic Games since 1972. Their ministry targets Elite to High Profile Players, -6 to +2.

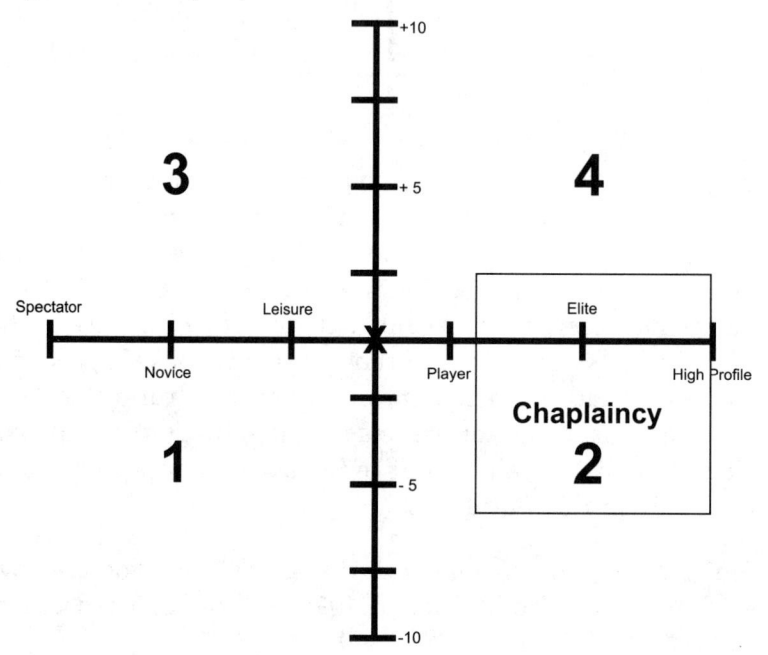

International Sport Conferences/Coalitions

The trend to hold international sports ministry conferences began in Hong Kong in 1984, with fourteen nations represented. This was the first time there was an intentional gathering of sports ministry people from around the globe. The International Sports Coalition was formed in 1986 as an outgrowth of the 1984 meeting. In 1990, the first regional coalition of sports ministries, the European Christian Sport Union (ECSU), was formed. Such conferences and coalitions have helped sports ministry become a worldwide movement by enabling sports ministry people to network, support, partner with and encourage each other.

In 1992, a partnership between Bible Societies, sports ministries, radio, internet, television, and other literature agencies began called, Major Sports Event Partnership (MSEP). The partnership seeks to strategize with and empower churches and believers in local communities around the world to share their love for Jesus in a simple and practical way during major sporting events. MSEP develops videos, literature, evangelistic brochures, CD-rom, and sport Bibles featuring the faith stories of High Profile believers who have participated in the major sport

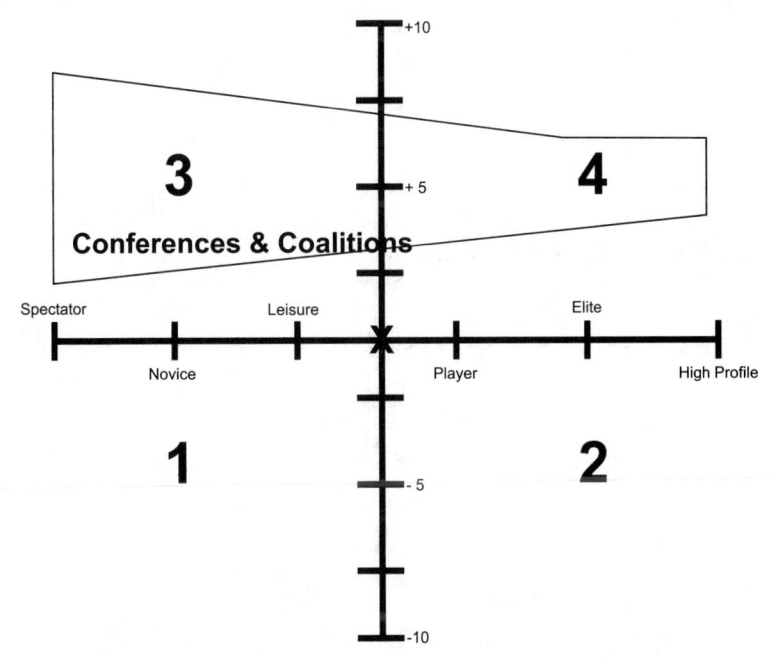

CHAPTER SIX

> Sports ministry has grown tremendously since 1988.

events to show in churches and believers homes as an outreach to their not yet believing friends and communities.

Sports ministry has grown tremendously since 1988. In that year thirty-five countries had established sports ministries. Eight years later, 1996, there were 90 countries involved in sports ministries. By 2003, there are over 150 countries involved in sports ministries and 40 regional coalitions are being developed to better serve the network of sports ministries worldwide.

Where are we in the world of sports ministry today? What new trends are evolving? Though it may be too early to predict some of the emerging ministry trends, there are two models that deserve our attention.

Sport Ministry Schools and Academies

There is an emerging trend to formally train people in sports ministry. The International Sport Coalition (ISC), in partnership with Sport for Christ Action South Africa (SCAS), has initiated a school specifically geared to train leaders in sports ministry. The International Sport and Leadership School (ISLS)

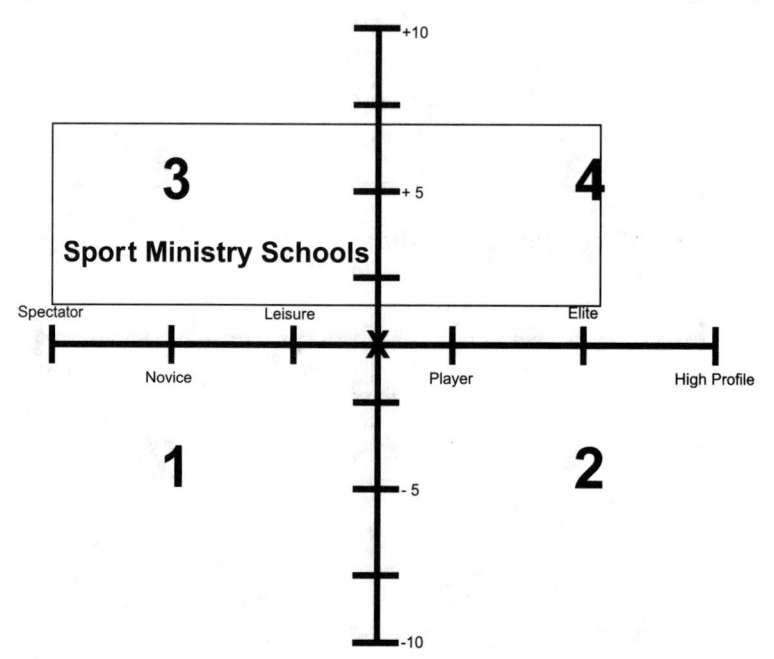

hosts a cadre of sports ministry leaders around the world to educate and train the next generation of leaders in sports ministry. The school enables new leaders to walk in the footsteps of sports ministry pioneers who have gone before and build on the foundations they laid. The ISLS is built upon a network of more than 150 Sports Ministry organizations through its association with the International Sport Coalition.

Sports ministry training is also being offered as a course of study at colleges and universities around the world. After a three-year pilot program, Sports Leadership and Intercultural Studies course (SLICS), developed in partnership between Christians in Sport (UK) and All Nations College, was officially birthed in 2002. The course focuses on training and equipping sports ministry leaders through twelve academic coursework modules and practical experience with different sporting organizations and clubs.[10]

Kids Games

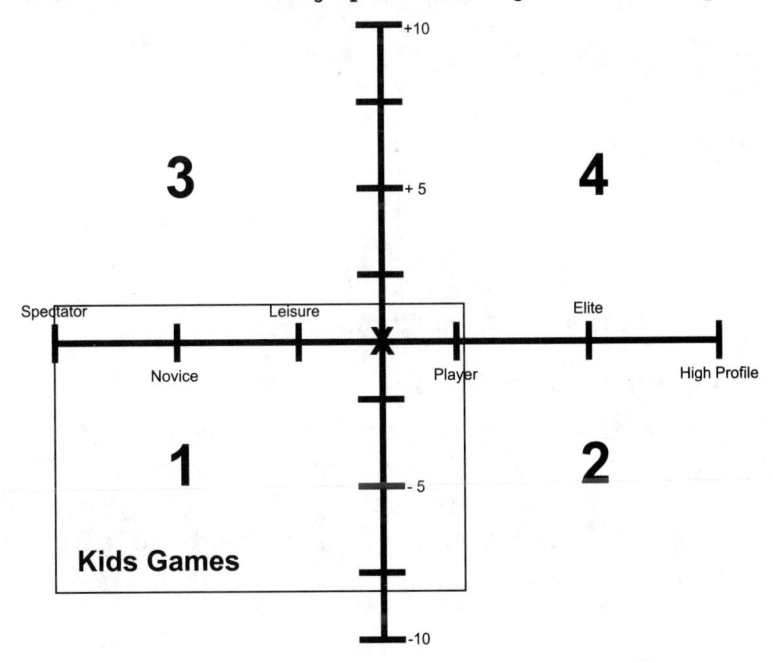

Kids Games is an outreach to children utilizing the attraction of games. It began in Spain as a church-planting strategy in the 1980's. In an effort by sports ministry leaders to respond to the blight of third world children, the Kids Games strategy was adapted to mobilize churches to reach the spiritual, recreational and humanitarian needs of children. The Kids Games movement was launched in the Mediterranean region in 2000 through a partnership of multimedia agencies, curriculum agencies, Bible societies and sports ministries. This collaboration provided the training, Bible studies, games curriculum and administrative structure for the Kids Games. Through a multi-day or -week format, the Kids Games program includes: opening and closing ceremonies, training, games, and Bible studies. Kids Games has a set program curriculum that has been used on every continent of the world. Following this same model Teen Games, and Family Games have emerged to reach older youth and families.

"Presence of Christ in Sport"

+ 10

Target audience to date

Spectator — Novice — Leisure — Player — Elite — High Profile

Where we are

− 10

"Presenting Christ through Sport"

Evangelism focus in sports ministry

Looking at the Map we can see an area of concentration of the target audiences of sports ministry in the past. The majority of the trends are located on the middle portion of the Map, indicating that the focus of sports ministry has been on evangelism.

Why has there been such an emphasis on evangelism? What caused ministries to focus solely on the middle portion of the Map? Modernity was an era that emphasized and valued the abilities to manage, control, quantify, and mechanize. The modern era shaped the gospel into something that could be measured and controlled. The priority and importance given to science played a huge role in influencing how to make the unknown known. It was believed that through science, humankind had the ability to know, monitor, quantify and control.

In an effort to know, control and quantify a person's change of allegiance, ministries minimized the *process* of someone coming to Christ, turning it into a decision or a single event. This decision could be made if you followed four steps. The decision also occurred at an exact date and time that could be recorded and documented.

> "...Modernity has infected evangelism with a zeal to motivate decisions...An attempt to motivate this response prematurely can quickly bring about misunderstanding, resentment and even a short-lived insincere faith."[11]
> -James Engel and William A. Dyrness, *Changing the Mind of Missions*

To quantify and monitor decisions made for Christ, ministries asked people to raise their hands or to walk an aisle so that they could calculate the number of converts resulting from each ministry event. The ministries were validated by the number of converts counted. Knowing the number of converts gave potential donors the information needed to make their decisions about whether to support a certain ministry organization. The idea of "more is better," influenced ministries to aim their focus on the majority of the people who were the easiest to reach; that is, they went after Spectators, Novices, and Leisure from a -3 to the midline.

> The modern era shaped the gospel into something that could be measured and controlled.

CHAPTER SIX

The importance placed on quantity caused ministries focused on Players, Elite, and High Profile to change their focus to Spectators through Leisure. Why? It was easier and quicker to reach more people on the left side of the map. The potential quality of Player ministry was replaced by the quantity of Leisure and Spectator ministry. The dividends were far greater when hosting a sport outreach event than when working tediously one-on-one with a High Profile player. The yield for effort is greater in quadrant 1 ministry than quadrant 2 ministry.

Some ministries have a desire to reach quadrants 2-4, yet the people who are doing the ministering are from quadrants 1-3. For example, sport chaplains or chapel leaders will use a sport concept or story to illustrate Scripture. Players, however, really desire and need to hear how biblical truth can be lived out in the activity of their sport experience. The approach clearly does not address the need. Sport is not valued as the place where life application takes place, but rather as the medium and vehicle for the gospel message to impact them spiritually.

The mechanization of the modern era also impacted sports ministry through the focus on pinpointing the exact time and cause of conversions, evangelistic programs that provided clear cut how to techniques of evangelism, and fill-in the blank Bible study aids.

The emphasis on evangelism and trivial value given to sport itself continued the divide between the sacred (saving souls) and secular (sport). This pervasive approach to sports ministry, where sport was simply a means to an end, fragmented the wholeness in which God created in humankind.

What can we learn from the history of sports ministry? In spite of modernity's infatuation with control, quantity, mechanization, validation, and knowledge, God continued to work out His purposes by glorifying Himself through sports ministries. Many people came to know and grow towards Christ and in Christ through the faithful obedience and efforts of the pioneers in sports ministry.

Yet a new millennium demands new ways of thinking. So, where do we go from here? What should the focus of sport in ministry be? Instead of continuing to replicate ministry trends and models, we need to reflect and learn from the past. We must be keen to the negative cultural values that could quietly seep into our perspectives, values and beliefs and, in turn, undermine the truth of the gospel. It is vital that we critically analyze the times in which we live to avoid the pitfalls and seize the opportunities this new era has to offer.

> A new millennium demands new ways of thinking.

Questions to think about:

1. Why didn't the Early Church influence the sport culture of the day? What could they have done to change the history of sport and sports ministry?

2. Think of the Christian fellowship and activities that you are involved in. Do these activities reflect the dualistic mindset that values "spiritual" activities more than "secular" activities such as sport?

3. Think of the sport experiences you have had or are currently involved in. Do these activities reflect the dualistic mindset that segregates "physical" activities by placing "spiritual" things on the sidelines or simply before or after games?

4. Many times we see Elite or High Profile players kneel briefly or make other religious gestures after they have made an important play in a game or match. Do you think such behaviors are effective ways to acknowledge God? Why or why not?

5. How has modernity influenced the sport ministries that you know?

6. What can we learn from the past that will help us to avoid cultural pitfalls and seize the opportunities that the new millennium has to offer?

The Focus of Sport in Ministry

CHAPTER SEVEN

What should the focus of sport in ministry be? What can we glean from history that will help us plan and strategize how to impact the world of sport for Christ? How can we best analyze and shape sport in ministry in the future? In this chapter we will consider how to answer these questions by describing four primary foci of sports ministry. We will use them in conjunction with the Sport in Ministry Map to identify what we call the *frontiers* of sport in ministry, and explore how best to reach the frontiers for Christ in our postmodern age.

Sport Ministry's Four Areas of Focus

Sports ministry to date can be divided into four main areas of focus:

+ Ministry *to* the people of sport[1]
+ Ministry *through* the people of sport[1]
+ Ministry *in* the activity of sport
+ Ministry *through service in* sport and *through* sport activity

Each of these areas can be incorporated into the same ministry but often one area takes precedence. Often ministries and churches stress a single approach, developing their

> People of sport can be described as an unreached people group. This is a group worthy of the gospel of Christ.

programs accordingly. The chosen focus of a sports ministry reveals more than the main focus of the ministry, it is a statement revealing what is most valued.

Ministry to the People of Sport

Before continuing, an important point of clarification is needed about the definition of the term "people of sport". To date, many sports ministries have broadly defined "sportspeople" as those who simply have an interest in sports or casually participate in sport activities. Such a group would include Spectators, Novices and Leisure people. Under this interpretation, ministry programs designed to introduce people to a sport, games for children, and leagues for leisure have been considered as ministries to the people of sport. The authors of this book, however, use the term much more narrowly to refer exclusively to Players, Elite and High Profile, quadrants 2 and 4, as determined by the perspective and mindset that they have toward sport. (Chapters 4 and 5 explained how to chart such players on the Sport in Ministry Map.) As mentioned before and will continue to be explored in the next chapter, there is a desperate call to minister to these people of sport in a well-balanced and integrated way.

People of sport can be described as an unreached people group. This is a group worthy of the gospel of Christ. People of sport, Players, Elite and High Profile, have unique characteristics and issues that they face, and we need to be sensitive to these as we help them to grow towards and in Christ. This group can be difficult to reach since, due to their irregular sport schedules, regularly scheduled meetings are difficult to plan. Their weekend schedules also compromise their availability to attend and participate in church activities.

> A player's unique circumstances have been expressed this way, "He is temporary to everyone but himself. To his fans, he is an ideal. To team owners and managers a commodity. To his competitors an obstacle. The tentative existence of an athlete (player) is as ancient as man being thrown to the lions for the entertainment of kings. He is disposable, and to survive knowing this, he must remain self-absorbed and motivated for his own reasons. The desire to win must be the outcome. That is the only permanent thing."[2]
>
> –author unknown

Ministry *through* the People of Sport

Another focus of sports ministry is ministry *through* the people of sport. From the beginning of the sports ministry movement, sport has been used as a "platform" for communicating the Gospel of Jesus Christ, predominantly through the faith stories of players and coaches who love Jesus. Ministry *through* the people of sport is primarily focused on the Spectators and youth that are attracted to the success and fame of sport celebrities and players. Since Spectators idolize Elite and High Profile players, they often have a receptive ear when a Christian High Profile player shares about their faith in Christ. Ministry *through* sport is the focus of most sports ministries.

While ministry through the people of sport can be an effective model of ministry, we need to be careful not to exploit the Elite and High Profile players simply to serve our ministry purposes. Some important questions to consider are: Do we only call or contact an Elite or High Profile player when we need something? Does the Elite player have the maturity and desire to share his faith story? Is he comfortable communicating to a large group?

Much emphasis on ministry through the sportsperson has developed around the use of top players of the country or on city clubs and teams. The responsibility/burden for ministry, however, is not limited to only the Elite and High

> While ministry through the people of sport can be an effective model of ministry, we need to be careful not to exploit the Elite and High Profile players simply to serve our ministry purposes.

Profile. In the US, the Fellowship of Christian Athletes, a secondary-and university-level school-based ministry has an outreach strategy for Players and coaches alike. These people of sport share the love of Christ with fellow students in "huddles" in over 7000 schools. Two other groups of Players who may not be High Profile, although they do compete at a semi-professional level, are The Korean Hallelujah Soccer Team and the US-based Charlotte Eagles and Lady Eagles. Both teams attract Spectators to listen as they share their love of Christ.

Ministry *in and through* the activity of sport

A third focus of sports ministry is ministry *in and through the activity* of sport. Natural walls of reserve that exist between people are broken down easily and quickly when they play sports together. The sport experience accelerates and enhances the ability to become friends, to see unveiled character and personality traits, and to build a strong sense of camaraderie.

Small group ministry can be divided into four states of development: history giving, affirmation, goal setting and community. Because of the camaraderie fostered in sport, people playing a sport together bypass the history-giving stage and start at the second stage, affirmation (through the sport experience). Consequently, sport activity can accelerate the small group development process. For example, because small group competition is a central part of Fellowship of Christian Athletes (FCA) the spiritual walls between participants at these camps come down in as little as 36 hours, half of the typical 72 hours required in other camp environments.

The relational connections that come about naturally through sport make ministry in and through sport the best way to minister to the people of sport. The following chapters will detail why this is true and discuss how ministry to the people of sport in and through the activity of sport will help restore the world of sport.

> The relational connections that come about naturally through sport make ministry in and through sport the best way to minister to the people of sport.

Ministry of service *in and through* sport activity

A fourth focus of sports ministry is the ministry of service *in and through* the sport activity. The activity of sport can be a basis in which the humanitarian needs of people can be addressed. Sport often serves as a rallying point to attract people to help in meeting these needs. Bikeathons, marathons, and golf marathons are examples using the enthusiasm of sport to heighten awareness of needs and raise funds to meet them. Hosting sport tournaments is another strategy to raise money for specific needs. Requiring donations of canned food items or cash as the price of admission to a sport to a sporting event is another means to gather food or funds.

International partnerships of good will are another strategy of the models of ministry in and through the activity of sport. For example, when a town in India lacked a well for drinking water, a cricket match between the national teams of England and India was held for the specific purpose of financing a well for this town through the ticket proceeds. In another example, Samaritan's Purse partnered with the Kids Games in Africa to give a shoebox filled with basic necessities to each participant. Likewise, during the civil war in Rwanda, ministries ran a soccer league in the refugee camps for the children. These are just a few of many partnership efforts to serve others in and through the activity of sport.

Foci of Sports Ministry and the Sport in Ministry Map

Each of the foci of ministry will be examined in relationship to the Sport in Ministry Map. This will enable us to see the areas on the Map that sports ministry has targeted up to the present time and will help identify the frontiers of sport in ministry.

The focus of ministry *to* the people of sport, in its broadest sense, has targeted mainly Spectators Novices and Leisure (Quadrants 1 and 3 on the Map) through sport programs and leagues from youth through adult. The approach used has been sport evangelism. Very few ministries have focused

> **Very few ministries have focused solely on Elite and High Profile and an even smaller percentage focus on Players.**

CHAPTER SEVEN

"Presence of Christ in Sport"

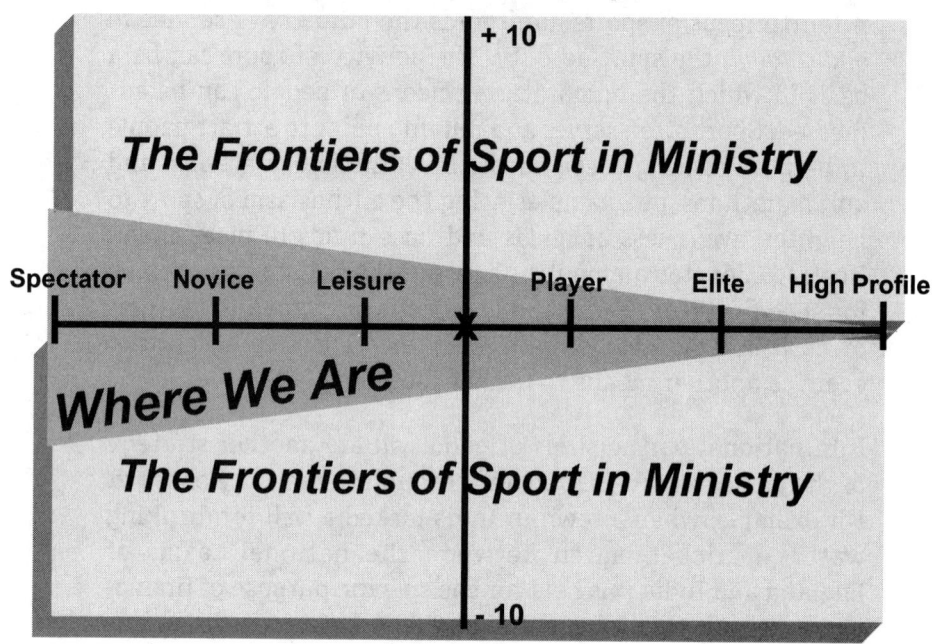

+ 10

The Frontiers of Sport in Ministry

Spectator — Novice — Leisure — Player — Elite — High Profile

Where We Are

The Frontiers of Sport in Ministry

- 10

"Presenting Christ through Sport"

> Ministry *in* and *through* the activity of sport and ministry through service in and through sport activity are the focus points of opportunities in the frontiers of sport in ministry.

solely on Elite and High Profile and an even smaller percentage focus on Players (Quadrants 2 and 4). The focus of ministry *through* the people of sport has been the most common approach to ministry, sport evangelism. Ministry *in* the activity of sport has been an area that, up to the present time, has not been fully explored. There are a limited number of ministries and resources that have effectively ministered to the heart of players to help them to grow in Christ in the activity of sport. This focus, has great potential for reaching people in Quadrants 2 and 4 on the Map. Ministry through *service in* and *through* sports activity has been an effective means of demonstrating the love of Christ and meeting humanitarian needs. This has been a wonderful way for people of sport to minister in a tangible way. The target audience of this focus is mainly Quadrants 1 and 3, but people of sport, Quadrants 2 and 4, are also included indirectly. Whenever people are able to help in life-threatening or crisis situations, it is not only the recipients that are blessed but the givers as well. Players able to minister to people are ministered and blessed in return.

The trends and foci of sports ministry when placed on the McCown Sport in Ministry map show us the target audiences of the sports ministries to date.

The sports evangelism approach used to minister to the people of sport and through the people of sport have targeted Quadrants 1 and 3 on the Sport in Ministry Map. The Map reveals that much more attention is needed to target the people of sport in quadrants 2 and 4. This is what we have identified as the frontiers of sport in ministry: the neglected group of Players, Elite and High Profile people. Ministry *in* and *through* the activity of sport and ministry through *service in* and *through* sport activity are the focus points of opportunities in the frontiers of sport in ministry.

Analysis of Sports Evangelism

It is important at this point to analyze the current state of sports ministry to help us think through how to effectively approach and minister to the frontiers of sport in ministry. Sports evangelism, the predominant approach to sports ministry, is an "outside-in" approach to ministering to the sports world for Christ. Traditionally, what is done in sports evangelism is to send believers from "outside" the world of sport, as missionaries "inside" the world of sport to evangelize. This has been an effective approach in sports ministry resulting in many people of sport changing allegiance and making a commitment to Christ.

While sports evangelism has had a positive impact on many people's lives, this approach has also had some negative repercussions. In many places in the world, when a person of sport has had a change of allegiance, he is encouraged to leave the sport world. Dualism, still alive and well in the church, sees sport as a negative influence, a bad environment, or just a waste of time for believers. The new believer is encouraged to stop playing sport and become involved in church life or in full time Christian work. Or more subtly, a believer in the world of sport is pressured to put church

> What would happen if all the believers in the world of sport stopped playing sport?

activities as a higher priority than her sport commitments, implying that one is of greater importance than the other. This idea of "capture and rescue," that is, "capturing" a person of sport and then "rescuing" them safely into the arms of the Christian community, has had detrimental effects on the people of sport, the sport community, and the world.

What would happen if all the believers in the world of sport stopped playing sport? What negative results would that have in sport and in a world that embraces sport? What would that say to the people of sport who have been wired by God to play sport? How will the people of sport be reached for Christ? Sport should be a place where people glorify God by enjoying and exercising the talents and abilities He has given them. The world of sport provides an environment in which believers participate alongside not yet believers, giving these people of sport, who love Christ, an "inside track" for developing relationships with Christ and demonstrating His love to their peers who do not yet believe. The Christian community should encourage people of sport who are believers to live out the presence of Christ in their sport environment, walking alongside to help and support them instead of trying to "capture and rescue" them out of that environment. The most effective way to reach the frontiers of sport in ministry is to help and support believers who are people of sport grow in Christ through the activity of sport. The frontiers of ministry call for an "inside-out" approach to ministry. People of sport who love Christ, "Insiders," inside the world of sport that naturally overflows "outside" as Spectators and others see the impact of Christ in the lives of the believers and on the sport communities where they live.

> **The most effective way to reach the frontiers of sport in ministry is to help and support believers who are people of sport grow in Christ through the activity of sport.**

> "A common misconception is that 'spending time with God' means being *alone* with him. Of course, as Jesus modeled, you need time alone with God, but that is only a fraction of your waking hours. *Everything* you do can be 'spending time with God' if he is invited to be a part of it and you stay aware of his presence."[3]
> –Rick Warren, *The Purpose Driven Life*

During Jesus' last days on earth He told his disciples, "...But you will receive power when the Holy Spirit comes on you; and you will be my witnesses in Jerusalem, and in all Judea and Samaria, and to the ends of the earth."[4] Jesus told the disciples to witness in their hometown of Jerusalem. The sports world for people in quadrant 4 is their "Jerusalem," it is where they "live." Often quadrant 4 people are asked to minister to quadrants 1-3 (all Judea and Samaria) though they are the most effective people who can minister to their Jerusalem—the frontiers of sport in ministry. Players, Elite, High Profile, trainers (coaches), sport psychologists, sport physiotherapists are "insiders" who understand the mindset, heart, and experience of people in quadrants 2 and 4. They are role models that can demonstrate, proclaim, experience and integrate the presence of Christ right on the field (pitch), court, and track through the sport experience. This is how transformation will take place in the frontiers of sport in ministry.

Sport in Ministry in Postmodern Times

As we seek to minister effectively to the frontier of sport in ministry, we need to consider the times in which we live. The age of modernity that influenced and shaped sports ministry is no longer the prevailing ethos today. New attitudes and emerging worldviews demand attention and thought. Simply changing the *approach (tactics)* to ministry will not impact the world of sport as much as a new way of *thinking* about sport in ministry. What issues will we need to think through in order to effectively serve the people of sport in the activity of sport? What ideas do we need to embrace and which ones do we need to be cautious about? What future direction must sport in ministry take in order to reach the frontiers that need it so desperately?

In contrast to the controlled, quantifiable, uniformity of the modern era, change characterizes the postmodern era. The definition for "normal" has been lost. Fortunately this atmosphere of change does not trouble the people of sport, who are used to change and flux. Situations, plays, teammates, opponents, officials, rules are constantly changing

> Players, Elite, High Profile, trainers, sport psychologists, sport physiotherapists are "insiders" who understand the mindset, heart, and experience of people in quadrants 2 and 4.

in the world of sport. What may seem like chaos to the non-sportsperson is an expected reality for the sportsperson.

> "It's not *whether* we do missions, it's *how* we do missions. It's following the biblical model. Rwanda is a great example: 80% of Rwandans claimed to be Christian, yet this is a country that in 1994 witnessed one of the most brutal genocides in history. Christianity was a veneer laid over tribal hatred. Discipleship appears not to have taken place. Numbers should not matter in missions, and numbers have been first in the modern missions movement. Numbers matter to marketing people. They should not matter to Christians. What we should do is obey Christ, do it exactly the way He said to, and develop a blameless, discipled, spiritually mature Church and let the numbers take care of themselves. Jesus took 12. He didn't use a mass-market approach, which is completely modern."[5]
> –Chris Simmons

Visual images and graphics are all vital to the postmodern mind. Where words were the point of reference in the modern era, visual images are the reference point now. Team logos, video clips of sport highlights, instant replay, slow motion replay are all a standard part of sport. From a sport in ministry standpoint, this emphasis on the visual gives us a much deeper opportunity to minister effectively through the demonstration of Christ in and through the activity of sport.

There is an intense spiritual hunger in the postmodern era. It is no longer a question of the existence of God, but which god? People are not interested in organized religion but very interested and intrigued with spiritual things. This means that they are open to trying Jesus to see if Jesus is true. They will want to see if biblical truth in their sport experience makes a difference or not. This opens doors for us to help them experience for themselves the presence of Christ not only in sport but all of life as well.

In the modern world things could be calculated knowing in advance what the trends would be. Things were black and white. In postmodernism there is a "double ring:" not "either-or" but rather "both-and." It is no longer enough to have either a large event outreach but it's necessary to have small group discussions as well. One size does not fit all any more.

Life is a serious of dramatic scenes, not a list of propositions. Postmodern men and women realize that they are a part of something bigger, yet they don't know what that something is. They are looking for a way to connect their story to a bigger story. This provides us the opportunity to share stories by exchanging our experiences. Everyone has a story, and the story of sin being played out in all of our lives has made us lose sight of "the story of ourselves, the story that tells us who we are supposed to be, and how we are supposed to act."[6] Listening to others' experiences while sharing our own allows us to talk about God's redemptive story being played out in our lives. Instead of merely hearing stories about sport, people of sport want to hear real-life experiences of sportspeople dealing with issues and experiences similar to the ones they themselves face. To meet the needs of the postmodern person of sport, we must utilize the narrative of sport experience instead of simply telling sport-related stories.

In summary, sport in ministry, is in many respects, more strategic now than ever because sport itself, rather than ministry models and programs, provides real-life experiences where change, visual stimulation, and a built-in community can naturally feed intense spiritual hunger. What better way to satisfy a spiritual appetite of the world of sport than the presence of Christ lived out in and through the people of sport in the activity of sport? Through relationship the people of sport who know Christ can demonstrate and help others experience and validate truth in the activity of sport. The next chapter unfolds this new way of thinking that sport in ministry must consider to effectively minister to the people of sport today and in the future. The activity of sport through

> Everyone has a story, and the story of sin being played out in all of our lives has made us lose sight of "the story of ourselves, the story that tells us who we are supposed to be, and how we are supposed to act."

believers inside the world of sport must be the focus of sport in ministry if it is to impact the postmodern sportsperson in a significant way.

Questions to think about:

1. Think about the sports ministries in which you have been or are currently involved. Which of the four foci of sport in ministry does each of these ministries fall under?

2. In addition to irregular sport schedules discussed in this chapter, what are some of the other distinctive characteristics and unique issues faced by people of sport and those who seek to minister to them?

3. In what ways has your sport experience influenced you toward or away from glorifying God in your sport?

4. If every believer currently involved in the world of sport left that world to participate solely in the faith world, would anyone notice their absence? If so, what would be the changes that we would notice?

5. Have you heard the saying, "Things aren't what they used to be"? Do you feel tension in your life or ministry because the current era in which you are living in differs markedly from what you are used to? What changes or accommodation will you have to make in order to effectively minister to the current generation?

6. Why is sport in ministry perhaps more strategic now more than ever?

Sport Development:
A New Perspective of Sport in Ministry

CHAPTER EIGHT

As people created in God's image, we are, by nature, relational creatures. After the Fall, all Creation seeks to be whole again—to be whole in our relationships with God, with ourselves, with others, and with all of Creation. As is true for relationships, all of sport likewise is in need of redemption. *Sport development ministry* seeks to bring about this restoration of sport each of the following areas—physical, spiritual, emotional, intellectual, and social. In sport development ministry, sport is not exploited for the sake of ministry, nor is ministry discounted for the sake of sport. Sport is not treated as a separate entity from ministry, but the two are viewed together—holistically—as one in sport development. Simply stated, sport development ministry takes an integrated relationship-based, sport-valued approach in ministry.

As stewards of God's creation, we seek to develop and transform sport and the people of sport to their God-given potential. The authors believe this is best accomplished *in* and *through* the hearts of the people of sport *from the inside out*. The power of the Holy Spirit at work in the hearts of

> **Sport development ministry seeks to bring about this restoration of sport in each of the following areas—physical, spiritual, emotional, intellectual, and social.**

sportspeople is capable of transforming sport at every level. In order to understand how to transform the sport culture, we will first look at how Jesus' ministered through relationships and then apply His model of ministry to sport development. Next, we will explore how this model of ministry is integrated in sport development through the people of sport. Lastly, we will see how sport development can restore sport.

The House

A simple diagram of a house helps illustrate the principles of sport development ministry. This house is built from the bottom up starting with a common ground, based on shared values and interests. The relationships forming the main section of the house are established from the shared values and interests and are represented by the pillars of the house. The roof is comprised of two lines equal in length, angled towards one other and supporting each other in the middle. Each line represents the story—life values, cultures, personalities, talents and experiences—that each person brings to the relationship. The point where these two lines meet illustrates where the stories intersect. Thus, the roof symbolizes a mutual exchange and shared respect between individuals. (To keep this simple the house drawn is a one-on-one relationship. Multiple relationships would be shown by multiple lines to comprise the roof.)

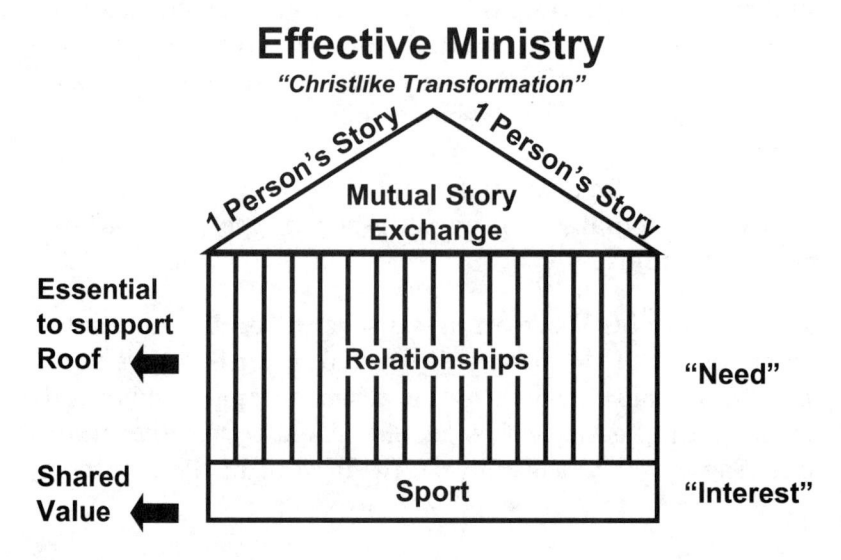

Effective Ministry
"Christlike Transformation"

- 1 Person's Story / 1 Person's Story — **Mutual Story Exchange**
- **Essential to support Roof** ← (roof)
- **Relationships** — "Need"
- **Shared Value** ← Sport — "Interest"

A Relationship-based Model for Ministry

Jesus effectively ministered to the needs of people He encountered. Whether it was physical illness, hunger, or death, He met people where they were, not at the exclusion or expense of their spiritual need, but prior to addressing their spiritual condition. We will examine how Jesus accomplished this in his interaction with a Samaritan woman at the well. The house illustration is patterned after Jesus' model of ministry. The story, found in John 4:1-42, is paraphrased from the Scripture text.

Tired from His journey, Jesus sits down by Jacob's well. A Samaritan woman comes to fill her water jug at midday when no other townspeople are around. Jesus, ignoring cultural taboos, asks the woman for a drink of water. Since Jews normally did not associate with Samaritans, the woman responds, "You are a Jew and I am a Samaritan woman. How can you ask me for a drink?" Jesus uses the opportunity to initiate a conversation. He says to her, "If you knew the gift of God and who it is that asks you for a drink, you would have asked Him and He would have given you living water." The starting point for their relationship is their common interest of and shared value for water.

> Whether it was physical illness, hunger, or death, He met people where they were, not at the exclusion or expense of their spiritual need, but prior to addressing their spiritual condition.

Effective Ministry
"Christlike Transformation"

| Water | "Interest" |

CHAPTER EIGHT

Having initiated a conversation about their common interest and physical need of water, Jesus now builds a relationship with her based on their shared value of water. Through the course of their continued conversation, Jesus touches her heart-felt need. Notice that Jesus does not immediately point out the fact that she is leading an immoral life nor does He condemn her. Instead, He focuses on showing care for her and what she needs. This allows for an open exchange of opinions and views. The woman is receptive to Jesus because He values who she is and listens intently to what she has to say. By remaining focused on her interests, Jesus meets her initially where she is, not where He wants her to be.

> **Having initiated a conversation about their common interest and physical need of water, Jesus now builds a relationship with her based on their shared value of water.**

Jesus treats the woman with value and respect and she, in turn, listens intently to what He has to say. Jesus asks her to bring her husband and come back. She answers that she doesn't have a husband. Jesus agrees, acknowledging that she has had five husbands and the man she is currently living with is not her husband. Attentive to what He has to say, she doesn't even flinch when Jesus reveals the truths He knows about her past and her present. Realizing that Jesus must be a prophet, she shares what she knows about the Jews and worship. Jesus responds by stating, "...the time has come when true worshipers will worship the Father in spirit and truth. God is spirit and His worshipers must worship in spirit and truth."

Effective Ministry
"Christlike Transformation"

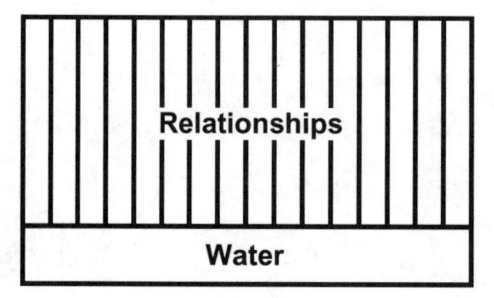

Relationships	"Need"
Water	"Interest"

She continues to dialogue freely with Jesus, saying, "I know that the Messiah is coming. When He comes He will be able to explain everything to us." She has heard the proclamation about the Messiah, but she has not seen or experienced the Messiah for herself yet. Jesus responds, "I who speak to you am He." Leaving her water jar at the well the woman goes back to her town and invites everyone to "Come, see a man who told me everything I ever did. Could this be the Christ?" There is a curious trust established and a life-changing connection between the Samaritan woman and Jesus. The dialogue involves a mutual respect and sharing of each other's values and views.

> This one woman's experience with the Messiah resulted in others experiencing and committing their lives to Jesus.

Because of this woman's encounter with Jesus, many Samaritans believed in Him. The story ends with the Samaritans saying to the woman, "We no longer believe just because of what you said; now we have heard for ourselves, and we know that this man really is the Savior of the world." This one woman's experience with the Messiah resulted in others experiencing and committing their lives to Jesus.

In this story, Jesus asks the woman questions, engaging her in conversation. Even though He is God, He doesn't lecture her. Jesus doesn't use this opportunity to put her down. Instead, He lovingly and patiently engages her in conversation. Her experience with Him indicates to her that He is authentic and trustworthy. He demonstrates care for her whole being—meeting her physical, spiritual, social, intellectual, and emotional needs. Jesus was interested in restoring all of her relationships—her relationship with Him, her relationship with herself (He transformed her old shame-based identity into a new identity in Him), her relationships with others, and with her relationship with all of Creation.

Sport Development House

In this one example of His interaction with the woman at the well, we plainly see how Jesus, during His time on earth, modeled effective relationship-based ministry. Unlike Jesus, however, our effectiveness in ministry often

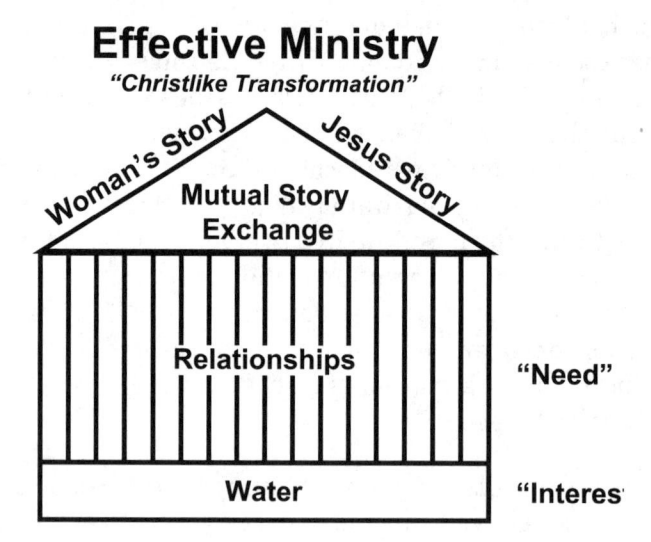

Effective Ministry
"Christlike Transformation"

- Woman's Story / Jesus Story
- Mutual Story Exchange
- Relationships — "Need"
- Water — "Interest"

> **In sport development ministry, the starting point in ministry is the common interest of sport.**

falls short of this model. Many times in sports ministry we feel the need to share the gospel of Jesus with others, yet we do not take the time to build relationships with the people we are ministering to. Seldom do we listen or give respect to their ideas and views about life because we know we are right in our thinking and they are wrong in theirs. We become so driven by our interest to share the gospel that we meet our own need without regard to theirs. So instead of an open exchange of ideas and values, our act of reaching out often becomes a lopsided relationship based solely on proclamation of the gospel without demonstration, experience and integration.

In sport development ministry, the starting point in ministry is the *common interest of sport*. Knowing that it is in the context of sport that the people of sport exist, feel most comfortable, and experience life most deeply, sport development values this common ground, recognizing that it is the place where relationships are built.

> "Coaching (training) is primarily about relationships. You don't coach disembodied 'players.' You coach individual young persons-persons with problems and hang-ups, ideas of their own (some good, some bad, some hard to tell), character strengths and weaknesses, parents (if they are one of the fortunate ones) who raised them permissively or strictly or somewhat in between, jokes to tell and sadness to bear, and dreams of glory and fears of disappointing."[1]
> -Jim Thompson, *Positive Coaching*

The pillars of the house represent the relationships that are built through shared sport experiences, suffering a terrible loss together, enduring difficult training periods, sitting out because of a nagging injury, going through times of poor performance, fear of inadequacy and failure, unfair criticism from the trainer, winning the league championship, or an undefeated season. These shared experiences, emotions and feelings enable us to empathize with their heartfelt needs and interests. If we meet people where their interests and needs are, it will give us entrance to their hearts. But in order to assess these needs, we must ask the following questions: What are sportspeople most passionate about? What are their heartfelt needs and interests? How can we lovingly and most appropriately serve them?

The goal of sport development is Christ-like transformation in the hearts of the people of sport, which, in turn, will bring transformation to sport. Transformation, however, can only occur in a relationship as each person brings and shares his or her own unique story comprised of each individual's culture, personality, opinions, values, talents, beliefs, experiences, and worldview. Just as the two friends support and learn from each other, so, too, do the two lines of the roof, provide both a protective covering and a support.

> **The goal of sport development is Christ-like transformation in the hearts of the people of sport, which, in turn, will bring transformation to sport.**

> "Evangelism is believing and living as if this is really good news, as if it's incredible news and we have something to say. It also means that we learned to say it the way Jesus said it and not just the way we want to say it. We have to learn his methods as well as his truth. So we learn to treat people with dignity."[2]
> -Eugene Peterson

Demonstrating the Gospel in Sport

In sport development ministry, a relationship-based, sport-valued approach effectively begins with the demonstration of the gospel in sport. We know that most people in our postmodern culture have to see something and experience it for themselves before they will believe it. They are not content to just take a statement "at face value". On the contrary, they believe that "actions speak louder than words." Similarly, when the first-century Christians were facing horrible abuse and ridicule for their faith, Matthew encouraged them to "...Let your light so shine before men that they may see your good deeds and glorify your Father who is in heaven."[3] For his audience, the best defense of their faith was the authenticity of the presence of Jesus in their lives apparent through their good deeds, as opposed to anything they might verbally communicate to their harassers. In spite of the mistreatment they faced, their Christ-like conduct would shine brightly through their circumstances.

It is true that the first step to ministry through sport development is demonstration, but this is not to say that the gospel does not need to be proclaimed. Through our normal interactions with the people of sport, we are able to both demonstrate and proclaim the presence of Jesus in sport. Proclamation is most effective in authentic dialogue with another. As described in the house section above, true conversation happens when the not yet believer shares his story and you share yours. Friends listen to friends. Just as Jesus respected the comments of the woman at the well we, too, can show love by respecting and welcoming the ideas of others. What issues are they dealing with in their sport?

> Through our normal interactions with the people of sport, we are able to both demonstrate and proclaim the presence of Jesus in sport.

What fears do they have? How are they performing? What is affecting their performance? Listening and showing an active interest for them will enable us to know where their hearts are.

Motivation for Sport Development

During Jesus' time on earth He demonstrated how to live a life reflecting God's glory. The strength of His ministry was based on His relationship to the Heavenly Father. His motivation was love. It is not enough to simply go around doing good deeds; rather, these deeds must be motivated by our love relationship to Jesus Christ. First, we must find our identity in Him and then in loving obedience we will be able to love our neighbors as ourselves.

Jesus teaches us to "Love the Lord your God with all your heart and with all your soul and with all your mind and with all your strength.' The second is this: 'Love your neighbor as yourself.'" He says that "There is no commandment greater than these."[4] In sport development, we are *ambassadors* of the great commandment, not just *doers* of the great commission. Previously in sports ministry, we have mistakenly given a greater priority to the great commission than to the greater commandment. The Apostle Luke stated, "Jesus grew in wisdom and stature, and in favor with God and men."[5] In much the same way, the whole sport development experience enables us to grow in love for God with our heart, soul, mind, and strength and in favor with God and others—in that order. Jesus tells us, "A new command I give you: Love one another. As I have loved you, so you must love one another. By this all men will know that you are my disciples, if you love one another."[6] Love is our identifying mark as believers. It must be what motivates us in the way we view and treat people.

> Love is our identifying mark as believers. It must be what motivates us in the way we view and treat people.

> "The way you relate to God...dramatically affects the way that you approach life. If God is only your *taskmaster* then you will feel that the Christian life, your relationship with Him, is a burden. If God is a *disciplinarian* then you will cringe when you err or become devious to try to avoid His anger. But if you first and foremost view your heavenly Father as *one who loves you* and wants to nurture you and guide you through life, then you know that the tasks and the discipline are for your own good. Once we take hold of our worth to God and His care for us, our new identity in Christ will affect the way that we relate to others...Reconciling us with each other was an essential part of Jesus' ministry. He broke through the barriers which separated the clean and unclean, the obedient and sinful...Jesus called to Himself those who, in the eyes of sectarians like the Pharisees, did not seem to have the necessary qualifications for fellowship with Him. In calling the despised to Himself, in eating with publicans, in restoring a fallen Samaritan woman, Jesus demonstrated that each could answer a call to fellowship with God *and* have a fellowship with each other."[7]
> -Michael Wilkins, *In His Image*.

Whole People

Sport development ministry values whole people. The authenticity of the gospel is that we live as whole people no longer fragmented and suffering from broken relationships due to sin. As we relate to sportspeople in and through sport we not only deal with their sport lives but *all* aspects of their lives. As restored people we have the ability to demonstrate wholeness in life as agents of transformation in all areas of a person's life. And as we help them grow in Jesus, we in turn grow as well. We are all in the process of growing either toward Jesus or in Jesus. We are all a part of a journey.

We have to be careful that we do not segregate spiritual life from other areas of life. To think that ministry only happens during a Bible study or on Sunday mornings inhibits us

---

The authenticity of the gospel is that we live as whole people no longer fragmented and suffering from broken relationships due to sin.

from promoting the integration of Jesus into all of our experiences—especially sport. The Apostle Paul encouraged Timothy, "...train yourself to be godly for physical training is of some value, but godliness has value for all things, holding promise for both the present life and the life to come."[8] Restated, physical training has value, but godliness has value for all things. Sport development ministry recognizes this, and integrates the value of physical training and training in godliness together. We have the opportunity to train for godliness as we train for sport!

There is a great opportunity to help the people of sport train to be followers of Jesus in the world of sport. Jesus enabled people to process things for themselves by asking questions. In fact, one of His customary teaching techniques was to respond to peoples' questions by asking another question. Jesus wanted them to think through issues for themselves. In this way, He pushed his listeners to the integration of their faith in real-life experiences. Jesus did not endorse a ten-step program on how to be a disciple, but rather focused on living out one's faith in the experience of life.

Accordingly, sport development, then, is not a program on how to do sport in ministry, but a way of thinking. Sport development releases the people of sport to be the people of sport by encouraging thought and reflection on the connection (integration) between biblical principles and how they relate and affect the sport experience.

> Sport development releases the people of sport to be the people of sport by encouraging thought and reflection on the connection (integration) between biblical principles and how they relate and affect the sport experience.

Development In and Through Sport

Development of sport occurs in the sport experience itself through the people of sport. That is, since most sports people have their identities wrapped up in their sport performance, they are very concerned about improving their sport experience. Their interests revolve around improving their sport skills and abilities: getting faster, gaining strength, refining skills, maintaining a good diet, and keeping up with the latest game trends and strategies. Sport development focuses on meeting these perceived needs by providing expertise and knowledge from sport professionals and players.

By becoming experts in the field of sport as trainers (coaches), physiotherapists, managers, sport agents, players and other sport professionals, we will be able to credibly build relationships based on the shared value of sport.

In the relationships we build we can not only demonstrate love and interest in what members of our target group care about, we, in turn, can also demonstrate through actions the love of Jesus. People of sport often have their identities wrapped up in their performance. The attention they get from Spectators and teammates is a salve on their shame-based identities. As people of sport strive to improve their shame-based identities through their performance we can demonstrate the freedom Jesus brings. Because of sin the identity of the sports person is racked with shame and guilt. They feel the same way Adam and Eve felt when they hid because they knew they were not living in obedience to the safety structure God set for them. What they thought would free them instead put them in bondage. What is the freedom that Jesus can bring to the people of sport?

> "There were days when I was nearly crazed with the fear of failure, when I would curse myself for the most miniscule mistake. Shame would sweep over me whenever I'd let my man score or I'd throw the ball away. Every time I played at one of our games and a substitute would come in for me I'd run to the sideline, head down, certain that I would never again be allowed on the court. With each tiny misstep, I would feel less and less part of the team and more and more isolated...'You're tougher on yourself then the meanest, most cantankerous coach in the world could ever be.' He'd lay his hand on my shoulder lightly, then added 'You're doing a great job. Just relax a little. If you keep working, everything will be all right. I suppose we'd say that Coach gave me self esteem...all I knew was that when nobody else thought I was worth the effort, he took an interest in me and made me feel that I had something valuable to offer."[9]
>
> -Lorraine Glennon and Roy Levitt, *Those Who Can...Coach*

Stewards of Sport

The parable in Matthew 25 illustrates the concept of good stewardship. A man entrusted three servants with his money while he went on a journey. Two of the servants took the money given to them to put it to work, while the third buried his money in the ground. When the master returned, the first two servants had doubled the investment they were given. The master was pleased with the servants and praised them, saying, "Well done, good and faithful servants! You have been faithful with a few things; I will put you in charge of many things. Come and share your master's happiness!" On the other hand, the servant who simply maintained what was entrusted to him was called "worthless" and thrown out in the darkness. Through this parable, we learn that stewardship involves increasing and multiplying the initial gift to its maximum potential. The expectation of the Master was that the servants would work to get a good return with what he entrusted to them. Servants actively engaged in making sure that the initial gift brought back good dividends were found to be faithful with the initial gifts, and, subsequently, were given even more.

Just as we are beings created by God, called to be stewards of Creation, as people of sport, we are therefore called to be stewards of sport. The Lord has given us the gift of sport and we need to be actively involved in doing whatever we can to not only produce a good return for the Master but to enjoy the opportunities we have to utilize the gifts. The reward for faithful servanthood is sharing in all that the Master has. This is what sport development ministry seeks to do: develop sport to its fullest potential. As stewards of Creation, we are called to restore sport and increase the dividends on God's initial investments! The power of the Holy Spirit active in each believer's heart can restore sport to its proper perspective and place in our world. To do this, however, we need people of sport who have had a change of allegiance to bring restoration to sport and the people of sport by infiltrating sport in every aspect and at every level. Players, trainers, sport psychologists, sport managers, sport physiotherapists, officials, sport committee members, rules

> Just as we are beings created by God, called to be stewards of Creation, as people of sport, we are therefore called to be stewards of sport.

committee members, and parents of sports people and other sport professionals are all called to be the embodiment of Jesus in their respective areas. Just consider the impact if this were to happen. What if trainers faithfully demonstrated Jesus to their teams and, consequently, the Players had a change of allegiance. The presence of Jesus lived out in their hearts would affect their behavior which, in turn, positively affect the behavior and attitudes of their opponents, the officials, and the game, all leading to the progressive restoration of sport to its full potential.

> "...The amazing truth of the gospel—the gospel of the kingdom—is that any person who comes to Jesus in faith receives a new life which begins in the heart and moves to transform the whole person. When the heart is surrendered to God, then the righteousness of any common disciple of Jesus surpasses that of the Pharisees because true righteousness begins on the inside. The Pharisees had a tendency to work from the outside in, expecting outward observance to produce inward change. That was why Jesus' most scathing criticisms were launched at the Pharisees, whose practice was to make the outside clean and beautiful, while their inner life—their connection to God—was dead. Jesus declared that the righteousness of the kingdom of heaven—that is, right living, right relationships, right actions—grow from the inside out. Personal transformation begins in the inner person through our understanding and response to the work of the Spirit of God, which then moves to produce change on the outside. We must develop an inside out mentality so that Spirit-produced growth of the inner person produces outward change and obedience." [10]
>
> -Michael J. Wilkins, *In His Image*

Jorge de Amorim Campos, "Jorghino," Brazilian professional futbol player, gives his personal account of how the integration of Christ in his life changed his behavior and enabled him to help demonstrate Jesus' love and then begin restoring sport. He says, "I used to be a 'bad boy' in Flamengo before. The referees may have got tired of showing me the red card as the most violent of all Flamengo defenders. But the peace I found for my spirit was so evident that it even changed the way I played soccer on the field. As a result, some years later the FIFA association granted me the "Fair Play" award as the world's most loyal soccer player—I had played in the German league for four seasons without ever receiving a single red card!"[11] As Jorghino testifies, sport development will not only transform the people of sport and the world of sport, but the individual believer. Sport development enables individuals to grow in Jesus by shaping every part of our lives into loving obedience and allegiance to Him. Being faithful holds possibilities of exponential proportions, eventually allowing His Kingdom to "come on earth"—through the world of sport—"as it is in Heaven."

> **Being faithful holds possibilities of exponential proportions, eventually allowing His Kingdom to "come on earth" through the world of sport "as it is in Heaven."**

CHAPTER EIGHT

Questions to think about:

1. How would you define an integrated relationship-based, sport-valued approach to ministry?

2. Why do you think Jesus spent time dialoguing with the woman at the well?

3. How can the gospel be demonstrated in and through the activity of sport?

4. In what ways have you incorporated "sharing stories" and exchanging experiences in your ministry techniques? Have you found use of the personal narrative of the sport experience to be effective?

5. We have proposed that development of sport occurs in the sport experience itself through the people of sport. How can the principles of sport development make a difference in how you approach sport in ministry?

Adjusting Our Sights to the Frontiers of Sport in Ministry

CHAPTER NINE

The sport experience provides moment-by-moment opportunities to demonstrate, proclaim, experience and integrate the reality and presence of Jesus. Yet to date, as discussed in Chapter 6, most of the trends of sports ministry have focused on reaching people classified along the midline of the spiritual continuum of the Sport in Ministry Map (see Chapter 4). Programs offered, materials written, and the messages proclaimed, have all been directed at people in the -2 to +2 range.

Sport development ministry allows us to depart from past trends, however. It provides the framework of thinking necessary for reaching the populations along the frontiers of sport in ministry. That is, through sport development, we can shift the ministry focus to quadrants 2 and 4. The new ways of thinking that grow out of sport development will help us effectively reach the frontier of sport in ministry. Sportspeople from a -10 to a -4 on the spiritual continuum can be effectively guided to grow towards Jesus, and we can assist people at a +4 and higher to grow in Jesus. In sport in ministry, while we encourage people to reflect the image of Christ in the activity of sport, we hope to transform the people of sport and the world of sport.

> **The sport experience provides moment-by-moment opportunities to demonstrate, proclaim, experience and integrate the reality and presence of Jesus.**

"Presence of Christ in Sport"

The Frontiers of Sport in Ministry

Spectator | Novice | Leisure | Player | Elite | High Profile

Where We Are

The Frontiers of Sport in Ministry

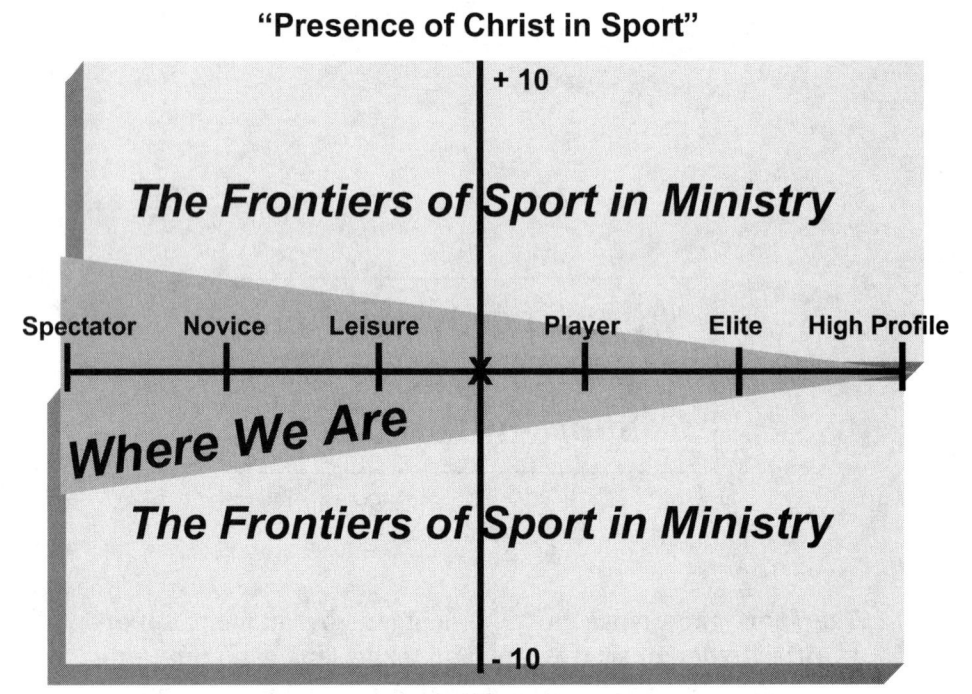

"Presenting Christ through Sport"

From Darkness Into Light

An examination of Plato's allegory, The Parable of the Cave, tells the story of human prisoners who have lived in a cave since childhood, unable to see out of the cave, their necks and legs chained in such a way that they can only see the wall of the cave straight ahead of them. Behind and above them is a fire that casts shadows of people walking by carrying various items onto the wall of the cave. Because they can neither move nor turn their heads, "reality" is based on shadows cast against the wall. If the prisoners are released from the cave and turn directly to the light outside, the light will painfully burn their eyes. They will need time for their eyes to adjust to light in varying degrees of brightness and intensity before they will be able to perceive anything at all. At first, they will only be able to look at things under the faint light provided by the moon's pale reflection. Once they are able to see images of things they have never seen before, they may deny that the new images are real. For some, the process of their reality being challenged is so painful they contemplate retreating back into the cave. Others begin to question their sense of reality since what they once thought was real no longer matches what they see. In time, their eyes adjust and they are able to see the sun and take in its light in its entirety. Ultimately, they come to appreciate the new images that the full sunlight enables them to see. Once they reach this point of adjustment, they see the truth (that is, the light) for what it really is and understand their proper place in relation to this new reality. They begin to make sense of the world around them as they literally see things in a new light.[1]

This parable describes a scenario similar to what occurs during the process of ministering to people in the frontiers of sport in ministry from a -10 to a -4 and +4 and higher. This can be seen in how the analogy of the prisoners in the cave parallels the process of evangelism of people found in the -10 to -4 range on the Sport in Ministry Map. People who are not yet believers are in spiritual bondage. They are imprisoned under the burden of sin and are spiritually blind to eternal truths. Their only perspective is formed from the dark shadowy images that they believe to be reality.

The activity of sport provides a way for not yet believers to exit the "caves" they presently inhabit because it serves as a common ground for sports people to interact. As the eyes of the former "prisoners" adjust to being around people of sport who love Jesus and radiate His image as they train and compete, they are able to see reflections of images they may never have seen before. As they see Jesus reflected by others, they may, at first, deny the new reality they see and defer to their previous ways of interpreting the world around them. Those of us engaged in sport development have the privilege of partnering in and witnessing their adjustment toward the light of Jesus. Adjustment of the eyes to His light and truth is not automatic; it is a process that will take time. Yet, oftentimes, ignoring the fact that it takes time to adjust old ways of

> **The activity of sport provides a way for not yet believers to exit the "caves" they presently inhabit because it serves as a common ground for sports people to interact.**

thinking to new, we ask not yet believers to immediately make a leap of faith from wherever they are on the spiritual continuum. Though an instant change can happen, it is highly unusual and our expectation is unreasonable. Instead, we need to be willing and able to walk with them through their period of adjustment from darkness to light.

Reaching people on the lower half of the Sport in Ministry Map. Oftentimes people who are between -10 and -8 on the spiritual continuum of the Sport in Ministry Map are antagonistic and belligerent toward believers. They do not appreciate having their perspectives challenged. They may even do things to intentionally undermine you and your ministry. Personally, it can be a very painful process to pursue someone who is antagonistically opposed to everything you stand for and who chooses to make fun of your beliefs. Nevertheless, having someone who is consistently focused on meeting their needs and interests and committed to demonstrating the authenticity of the gospel every day, on and off the pitch (field), is vital to their adjustment to truth. To prepare yourself to reach this frontier in ministry, you will need to think through your answers to the following questions:

- ✛ How can you be a caring teammate or trainer (coach) to people classified as a -10?
- ✛ How do you build a relationship with them?
- ✛ How do you allow the loving characteristics of Jesus to be exhibited through you in the way you train, without making them more antagonistic towards you?

Elite Players classified at -8 on the spiritual continuum will be cautious in their interactions with you; skeptical about you and your beliefs. They are struggling with competing realities of what they once knew to be true and now new possibilities of Jesus' truth. They might be fearful of where this new way of thinking might lead them. Their struggles are largely internal, making it difficult for others to see that they are in inner turmoil. Reflect on how you can help alleviate this internal struggle they are feeling. How will you demonstrate wholeness and redemption to them in the activity of sport?

Players at a -5 on the spiritual continuum are in the process of gradually turning to the light of Christ. For perhaps the first time in their lives, they are seeing and experiencing things that are in stark contrast to what they held to be true in the past. They are not antagonistic, but somewhat more comfortable with exploring and turning toward the truth. But for this to happen, they need to experience the truth of the gospel for themselves. Think through how you can help them experience biblical principles through sport. How can you help them experience the reality of Christ during training and in competition?

Reaching people on the lower half of the Map requires new approaches and different ways of thinking about ministry. The relationships built through sport will take time to develop—based on how quickly or slowly the "eyes" of the not yet believers adjust to the truth you are demonstrating. And although the adjustment process may be very slow and, at times, painful, take heart. For any demonstration of the reality of Jesus in your sport activity is a valid ministry. In sport development, progress cannot be measured by the one-time event of a conversion experience. It, instead, must be based solely on their adjustment to the Light.

Reaching people on the upper half of the Sport in Ministry Map. For sportspeople located on the upper half of the spiritual continuum of the frontiers of sport in ministry (those at a +4 or higher), we must consider how we can effectively provide challenges and opportunities for their spiritual growth. Interpreted for this context, Plato's Cave analogy reveals that people growing towards Christ need people to partner with them and walk patiently by their side during this process. As "insiders," who share the common story of sport, sportspeople who are already believers at +4 and higher can be those partners. They have the opportunity to demonstrate the Truth of the gospel in the

> **For any demonstration of the reality of sport Jesus in your sport activity is a valid ministry.**

context of the common story of sport. One of the characteristics of a person plotted as a +5 on the Map is spiritual reproduction. So, a person who has an intimate relationship with Jesus should be effectively ministering to those who are not yet believers. How can a mature person of sport in Christ be an agent of redemption to the people of sport? How should the attitudes and behaviors of a believer transform those around her?

Release to the Captives

The Cave analogy also reveals that, after release from the "Cave," under the new "Light," cultural perspectives and views once thought to be true may now represent nothing more than an imprisoned way of thinking. For example, although the ancient Greek culture had a huge impact on sport, the Early Church did not. Its believers were either too timid or not involved in sport at all to challenge the predominantly held views of the day. Where was the example of truth in sport to contradict the dualistic thinking that we are *whole* beings made in God's image, not *divided* into sacred and secular parts?

> **Placing Jesus at the center of all our activities is the solution to fragmentation and shattered lives.**

Thus, in our times, we must also combat cultural perspectives that are not in line with the truth. The "disconnect" often made between God and sport, faith and sport, church and sport, ministry and sport, needs to be reconnected and held to its proper biblical perspective. God values sport and the people of sport. The sportsperson can fully and seamlessly glorify God with her whole being in and through the activity of sport. To "reconnect" the "disconnect," sport in ministry must be totally integrated in the sport experience. The demonstration, experience, and integration of the gospel in the activity of sport is as valuable as proclamation of the gospel. Sport development seeks to view sportspeople as persons valued for their wholeness. Since this is the case, we need to think of ways to integrate faith seamlessly into our sport experience and connect God to all aspects of our lives—on and off the playing fields. The issue is not a matter of offering more Bible studies or simply praying before and after every game. This will lead only to the further segmentation and fragmentation in our sport experience, thereby excluding Christ from the whole. Although we have learned to think of our fragmented lives as reality, this is merely a behavior pattern we must unlearn. Placing Jesus as the center of all our activities is the solution to fragmentation and shattered lives. Restoration of broken lives can only come from Him. Likewise, restoration of sport happens through the hearts of the people of sport who know Jesus and reflect His image.

> "It is an undeniable fact that God's absolute power over His creation opens up endless possibilities for the Church to be active in the world. To deny this by saying the world and its cultures are owned lock, stock, and barrel by the devil is a cop-out. God reigns. God rules. And God expects nothing less than for His Church to reign and rule with Him. That the sovereign God is all-powerful over all of life compels His followers to bring 'every thought captive' to Christ. Until we do, our job remains incomplete."[2]
>
> -John Barber, *Earth Restored*

Isaiah 42:5-7 says, "This is what God the Lord says-He who created the heavens and stretch them out, who spread out the earth and all that comes out of it, who gives breath to its people, and life to those who walk on it; 'I the Lord, have called you in righteousness; I will take hold of your hand. I will keep you and will make you to be a covenant for the people and a light for the Gentiles, to open eyes that are blind, to free captives from prison and to release from the dungeon those who sit in darkness.'"

It is time that the people of sport bring release to the captives, freeing the "prisoners" from the "caves" and "dungeons"! We are released to be the people of sport that God intended us to be. We are released from the captivity of thinking that sport is evil and is not a productive way to

We are released to be the people of sport that God intended us to be!

spend time and energy. We are free to be a Light to the people of sport. The Lord who gives breath and life has released us to be the sports people He created us to be:

- ✣ Sport is a gift that God has given us to enjoy, a gift that fully utilizes our whole beings.
- ✣ When we play sports we are fully alive giving glory to God for the way He designed us.
- ✣ We can strive for excellence in our sport experience and bring glory to Him in the way we play.
- ✣ We give testimony to God through our play! We no longer have to think the only way we can witness for Jesus is by verbally testifying. Rather, *how* we play our sport is just as critical as *what* we say about Jesus.
- ✣ We demonstrate the presence of Jesus in the world of sport when we allow Him to use us to be agents of redemption, restoring not only the people of sport, but sport itself.
- ✣ We are free to be the people of sport to minister to other people of sport. Quadrant 4 people can and should be the ones to minister to other sportspeople!

In conclusion, we are free to be agents of redemption in the world of sport and free to transform the people of sport from the inside. Sport development is a way of thinking to release the people of sport to be the people of sport. Sport in ministry is not based on *what* we do but *who* we are. Sport in ministry is not a public display of conduct or a program but a vibrant relationship with Jesus that flows through the power of the Holy Spirit working in believers from the inside out.

People of sport, may you be empowered by the Holy Spirit to demonstrate the reality of Jesus in your sport activity. May the way you play be a bold vibrant statement of the Glory of God.

Sports ministry people may your ministry and influence with the people of sport release them to play, serve and minister in the world of sport to the glory of God.

The following scenarios are posed to help the people of sport who love Jesus to think through how to integrate their love for Jesus in all aspects of their sport experience. These scenarios are written generically to include all sports people who are believers. In each scenario, take the role of a Player, Elite, High Profile, coach, physiotherapists, manager, or sports ministry person to think about how the Kingdom of God can be demonstrated in each situation.

For each scenario answer the following questions:

- ✛ What are the emotions this person is feeling?
- ✛ What is his/her heartfelt need?
- ✛ Which biblical principles can you demonstrate to meet their need?
- ✛ How can you reflect the presence of Christ in this situation?

Questions to think about:

1. You are a teammate of a Player who is a -8 who has just seriously injured his knee.

2. Your team has just won a contest in double overtime!

3. You are a parent of an Elite player who is a +2. Every time there is a bad call he loses his temper at the officials.

4. You are a physiotherapist serving a Players, -4 , who is severely injured.

5. Your teammate, -6, has been training hard but not getting much playing time.

6. The trainer (coach) -5 constantly yells at your teammate, -2, for making mistakes.

7. You have just lost to your rival opponent in sudden death. How do you bring restoration and healing to your team, -6 to -8?

8. You are a chaplain to a professional team. How do you interact with a High Profile Player, -4, who is having his worst season ever?

9. The church where you work wants to begin a sports league for Players in the neighborhood -8 to -4.
   Where do you begin?

Appendices
Case Statements • Chapter 5

McCown Sport in Ministry Map-Engel Scale

y

3   4

S   N   L   P   E   HP

x

1   **Church Basketball Clinic**   2

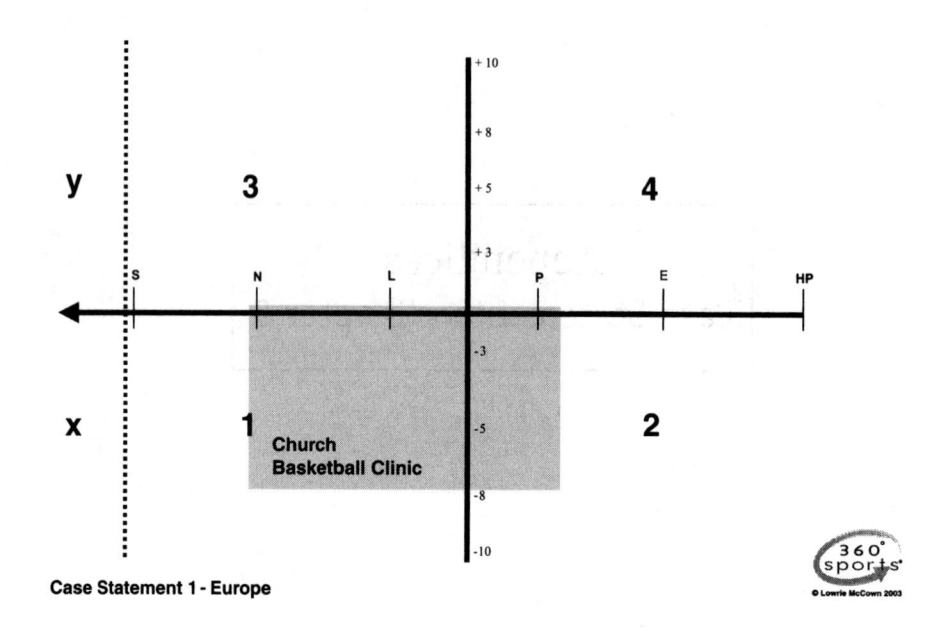

Case Statement 1 - Europe

McCown Sport in Ministry Map-Engel Scale

y

3   4

S   N   L   P   E   HP

x

1   **Street Children Basketball League**   2

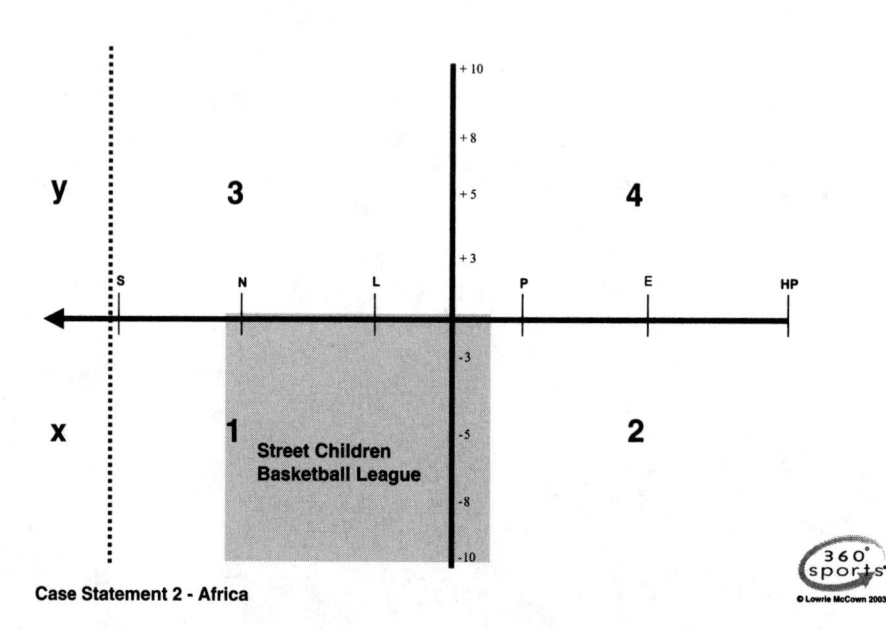

Case Statement 2 - Africa

APPENDICES / CASE STATEMENTS — 175

McCown Sport in Ministry Map-Engel Scale

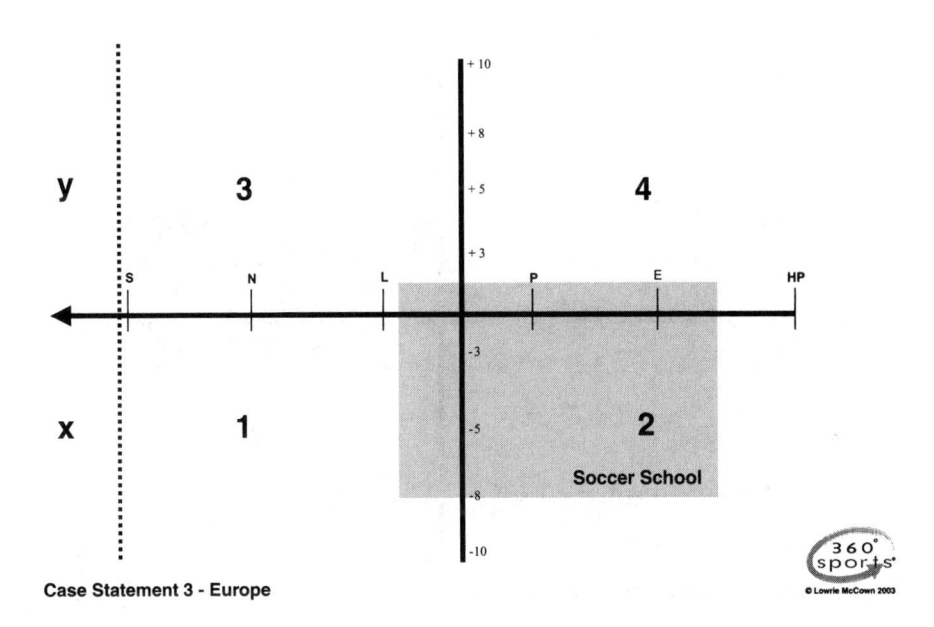

Case Statement 3 - Europe

(Soccer School)

McCown Sport in Ministry Map-Engel Scale

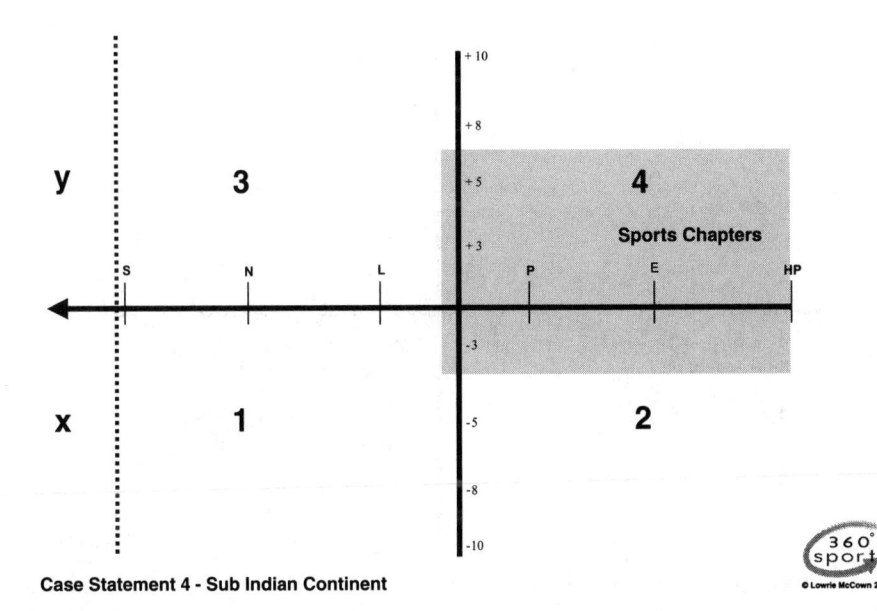

Case Statement 4 - Sub Indian Continent

(Sports Chapters)

McCown Sport in Ministry Map-Engel Scale

y | 3 | +10 / +8 / +5 | 4
S   N   L   P   E   HP
Tuesday Soccer Church

x | 1 | -3 / -5 / -8 / -10 | 2
Church Soccer League

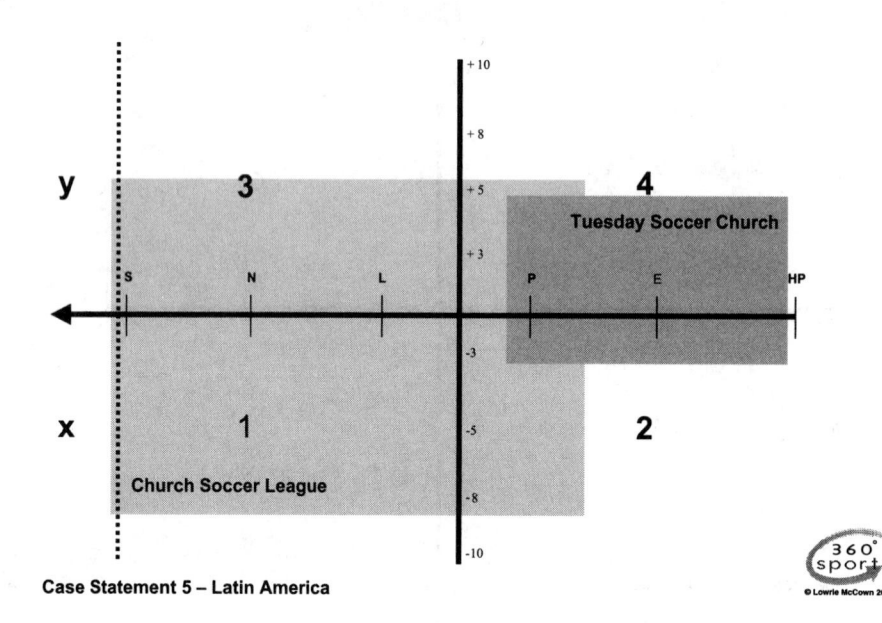

Case Statement 5 – Latin America

McCown Sport in Ministry Map-Engel Scale

y | 3 | +10 / +8 / +5 / +3 | 4
S   N   L   P   E   HP
Pro Soccer Team - Impact on Fans | Pro Soccer Team - Impact on Other Players

x | 1 | -3 / -5 / -8 / -10 | 2

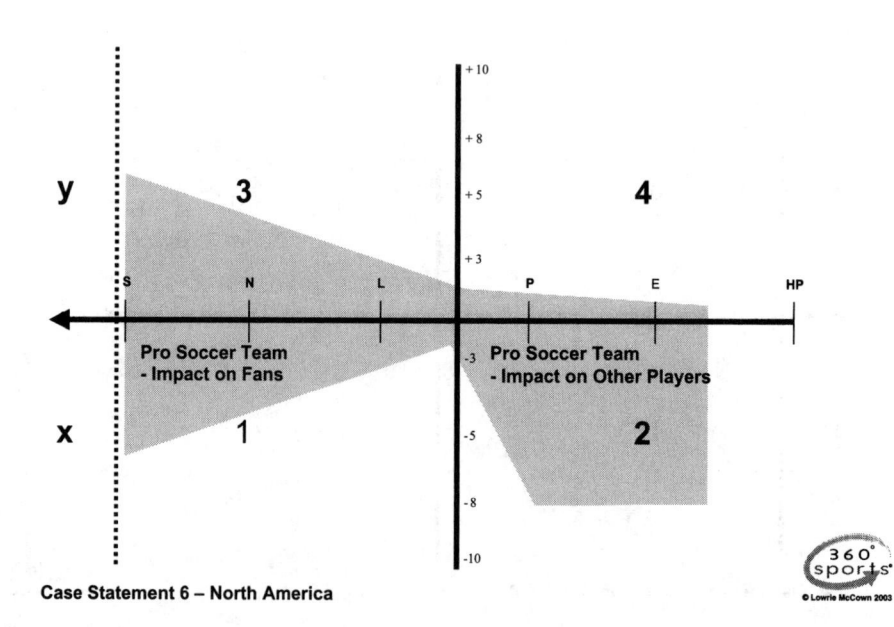

Case Statement 6 – North America

Notes

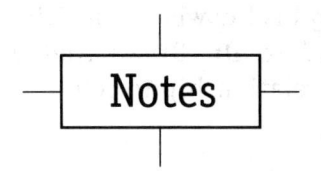

CHAPTER ONE

1. The British Sports Council
2. Adapted from *SPORT a Cultural History* by Richard D. Mandell, Columbia University Press, New York, 1984, (pgsvi,xvii,xix)
3. Valerie Gin, unpublished document, 2002
4. Richard Lipsky, *How We Play the Game.* Boston: Beacon Press, 1981 pp.5,11
5. Neal Offen, quoted in Richard Lipsky, *How We Play the Game.* Boston: Beacon Press, 1981 p.9
6. Angela Lumpkin, *Physical Education and Sport*, Boston: WCB/McGraw-Hill, 1998. pp.146-171
7. Thomas Tutko & Jeremy Thatcher. *Sport Psyching*, Putnam, New York, 1976, p.23a,b
8. Romans 8:20
9. Psalm 139:13
10. Iraneus of Lyons
11. John 1:14
12. N.T. Wright. *Colossians and Ephesians*. Grand Rapids: Wm. B. Eerdmans Publishing Company, 1989. p.77

CHAPTER TWO

Special thanks to Val's Gordon College colleagues, Dr. Marvin Wilson for sharing his knowledge of Hebrew culture and the early Church and to Dr. Bryan Auday for his insights concerning one's relationship to self.

1. I Timothy 4:8
2. I Corinthians 9:24-27; see also Acts 20:24, Galatians 2:2 and 5:7, Philippians 2:16 and II Timothy 4:7-8
3. Colossians 1:16-17
4. Genesis 1:26-27
5. Isaiah 43:7
6. Psalm 8:5-6
7. John 15:15
8. Genesis 2:25
9. Genesis 2:18
10. Genesis 1:28a
11. Genesis 1:28b
12. Genesis 1:29
13. Genesis 2:15
14. Genesis 2:16-17
15. Genesis 3:4-5
16. Genesis 3:6-7
17. Genesis 3:9-10
18. Isaiah 42:8
19. Genesis 3:7
20. Genesis 3:9
21. Genesis 3:9-12
22. Larry Crabb, *The Silence of Adam*. Grand Rapids: Zondervan, 1995.
23. Genesis 4
24. Genesis 3:16a
25. Genesis 3:17
26. Genesis 3:17-18

NOTES

27 Romans 8:22
28 Romans 5:6
29 Galatians 3:22
30 Ephesians 2:1
31 Colossians 1:17
32 John 1:1-2,14
33 I Peter 1:18-19
34 Bradshaw l. Frey, William E. Ingram, Thomas E. McWhertor, & William David Romanowski, *At Work and Play*. Ontario, CANADA: Paideia Press Ltd., 1986. p.41
35 Romans 6:23
36 John 3:16
37 II Corinthians 5:14-17
38 Romans 6:4, II Corinthians 5:17
39 II Corinthians 3:18
40 John 13:34-15
41 II Peter 1:22b
42 Colossians 1:16b-17;2:9-10
43 Frey et al., pp.98,105
44 Donald Sloat, *Growing Up Holy and Wholly*. Brentwood, TN :Wolgemuth & Hyatt Publishers, 1990. p.63
45 Acts 17:28
46 Colossians 3:9-10
47 I Peter 3:15
48 Colossians 3:12-13
49 I Timothy 4:4
50 John Fischer, *What on Earth are We Doing?* Ann Arbor: Vine Books Servant Publications, 1996. pp.92-93

CHAPTER THREE

1. Martens, Rainer. *Coaches Guide to Sport Psychology*. Champaign, IL: Human Kinetics Publishers, 1987. p.55
2. Swen Nater quoted in Andrew Hill's, *Be Quick-But Don't Hurry!* New York: Simon & Schuster, 2001. p.97-98
3. I Thessalonians 2:8
4. I Thessalonians 1:4-7
5. Andrew Hill with John Wooden, *Be Quick-But Don't Hurry!* New York, NY: Simon & Schuster 2001. p.96
6. John 7:38
7. John Eldgredge, *The Sacred Romance*. Nashville: Thomas Nelson Publishers, 1997. p.8
8. I Thessalonians 1:5b-7
9. Oswald Chambers, *My Utmost for His Highest*, Grand Rapids: Discovery House Publishers, 1992. August 30
10. ibid, July 23
11. ibid
12. J. W. Gardner, quoted in Donald Ray Haas', "Self Renewal in a New Century's Resolution," *www.advisortoday.com*, p.4

CHAPTER FOUR

We are extremely grateful to Dr. James Engel for his visionary work in describing the evangelism and discipleship process. The Engel Scale has had a profound impact on the creation and development of the Sport in Ministry Map. Thank you, Dr. Engel for your clear insights that have challenged and broaden our perspective on sport in ministry.

1. James Engel and William Dyrness. *Changing the Mind of Missions*. Downers Grove, IL: InterVarsity Press, 2000. p.101
2. Eduardo Galeano, *Soccer in the Sun and Shadow*. New York: (ISBN 1-85984-230-5) 1999. p.7-8
3. Andre' Oosthuizen. *They Once Had Horns A Rugby Fan's Recollections*. Hout Bay South Africa: Riverside Publications, 2003. from backcover

NOTES

4 Shirl Hoffman. *Sport and Religion*. Champaign, IL: Human Kinetics Publishing, 1992. p.243

5 George Selleck. *How to Play the Game of Your Life*. South Bend, IN: Diamond Communications, 1995. p.6c

6 Galeano, p.3

7 Selleck, p.4-5

8 Galeano, p.5

9 Sport Illustrated.com June 4, 2003

10 John Lucas quote in Selleck, *How to Play the Game of Your Life*. South Bend, IN: Diamond Communications, 1995. p.3a

11 Dave Cowens, ibid. p.4b

12 Bill Bradley. *The Values of the Game*. NY: Artisan, 1998. pp.16-17

13 I Corinthians 9:24

14 Engel and Dyrness, *Changing the Mind of Missions*. Downers Grove, IL: InterVarsity Press, 2000. pp.101-102

15 John 11:4

16 John 11:15

17 John 11:21

18 John 11:25

19 Mark 16:3

20 Mark 16:4

21 Matthew 28:2

22 John 11:43

23 John 11:44

24 John 12:1-2

25 John Barber, *Earth Restored*. Ross-shire, UK: Christian Focus Publications, Ltd., 2002. pp.32-33

CHAPTER FIVE

1. Curtis French. *More Winning Words Devotions for Athletes*. Waco, TX: Word Publishers, 1983. p.97–98
2. *The Player*. 360° Sports®. To be published in 2004.

CHAPTER SIX

1. I Corinthians 9:24-25
2. Oscar Broneer, "The Isthmian Games" www.ioa.leeds.ac.uk
3. John Stott, from John Stott's Issues Facing Christians Today, revised and enlarged edition, Collins/Marshall Pickering, 1990, as collected in Authentic Christianity/From the Writings of John Stott, compiled by Timothy Dudley-Smith, InterVarsity Press, 1995.
4. www.ymca.net/about/cont/history.htm
5. famers/Naismith.htm, *www.hoophill.com/halloffamers/Naismith.htm*
6. Tony Ladd & James A. Mathisen. *Muscular Christianity*. Grand Rapids, MI: BridgePoint Books, 1999. p.82-83
7. Don Odle, phone interview, November 1, 2001
8. *www.csrm.org*
9. Christians in Sport Annual Report 2003
10. ibid
11. James Engel & William A. Dyrness. *Changing the Mind of Missions*. Downers Grove, IL: InterVarsity Press, 2000. pp.100-101

CHAPTER SEVEN

1. Special thanks to Ashley Noll for the terms "ministry to the people of sport" and "ministry through the people of sport" from an unpublished document.
2. Author unknown, *Don't Let Your Fears Stand in the Way of Your Dreams*. New York: No Fear., Warner Books, 1995.
3. Rick Warren. The Purpose Driven Life. Grand Rapids, MI: Zondervan, 2002. p.88

4   Acts 1:8

5   Chris Simmons, A forum with Carlos Aguilar, Vincent Bacote, Andy Crouch, Catherine Crouch, Sherri King, and Chris Simmons. "The Anitmoderns," Christianity Today, November 13, 2000.

6   Leonard Sweet. SoulTsunami. Grand Rapids, MI: Zondervan Publishing House, 1999, p.425

CHAPTER EIGHT

1   Jim Thompson, *Building Character and Self Esteem Through Sports*. Portola Valley, CA: Warde Publishing, 1995. p.xi

2   Eugene Peterson, Taken from *A Conversation with Eugene Peterson*. by Michael J. Cusick, Mars Hill Review (3), 1995. pp.73-90

3   Matthew 5:16

4   Mark 12:30-31

5   Luke 2:52

6   John 13:34-35

7   Michael J. Wilkins, *In His Image*. Colorado Springs: NavPress Publishing Group, 1997. p.80-81

8   I Timothy 4:7-9

9   Lorraine Glennon & Roy Levitt, *Those Who Can...Coach*. Berkley, CA: Wild Canyon Press, 2000. pp.4-5

10 Wilkins, p.80-81

11 Jorghino, www.thegoal.com

CHAPTER NINE

1   Plato. "The Parable of the Cave." Taken from Os Guinness, *The Journey*. Colorado Springs, CO: NavPress Books, 2001. p.31-35

2   John Barber, *Earth Restored*. Ross-shire, UK: Christian Focus Publications, Ltd., 2002. p.29

360° sports© is a nonprofit* ministry committed to nurturing the heart of the player by training, connecting and providing educational resources for leaders to inspire the presence of Christ in sport and life.

Our Purpose is to assist athletes and coaches (the people of sport) at every level in developing whole, healthy restored lives. **Our Goal** is to train sport leaders, sport ministry leaders and parents to live and teach integrated Biblical principles, in sport, fostering whole life development and maturity in the player and coach.

360° sports© builds on the fabric of sports to bring the practical expression of Biblical truth to real-time sport and life. The result is whole life-on-life evangelism and discipleship through coaching and mentoring relationships that are centered fully in Christ and fully on sport.

* 360° sports© is an independent, 501.c3 non government organization (NGO) established in 2003, birthed out of the Fellowship of Christian Athletes Global Ministry to uniquely serve the integrated biblical development of the people of sport worldwide, operating out of offices in Marietta, GA, USA.

360° sports© is dedicated to the people of sport worldwide, transformed in Christ, so that when they play, people see Christ in them.

We focus on the development of the whole person of sport through biblical integration into the whole sport experience. Our passion is to see whole people of sport who transform whole teams, in the whole of sport, impacting whole communities throughout the whole world.

188

360° sports

VALUES

We value sport because we believe God values all creation and people including sport and its people.

We acknowledge that the word of God speaks directly to the heart and issues of the people of sport empowering them to become the people of God in sport.

We believe in collaborating with and resourcing the expansion of ministries and leaders who serve and influence in the world of sport as representatives of the global Kingdom of God.

We celebrate the diversity of cultures, sport, talents and function so that each culture can apply the principles to their particular need, styles and context.

We affirm that God is at work in the "not-yet believer" as powerfully as he is at work in the "believer."

We seek to be "New Wine" by bringing fresh biblical insights to the diverse "Mosaic" World of Sports by serving with the sport community with informational and relational integrity.

360° sports

Reaching the hearts of players around the web and around the world

www.360sports.net

360°sports© participates in a world wide movement comprised of leadership in over 800 organizations in more than 160 countries. As a leader in this movement, we emphasize spiritual transformation within the hearts of sport participants through training, mentoring, networking and resources.

Visit us at **www.360sports.net** for additional resources.